Nita Mehta's
Soups & Salads

Nita Mehta's
SOUPS & SALADS

Nita Mehta

B.Sc. (Home Science), M.Sc. (Food and Nutrition)
Gold Medalist

ANU KSHETRAPAL
TANYA MEHTA

SNAB
Publishers Pvt. Ltd.

Nita Mehta's

SOUPS & SALADS

© Copyright 2004-2006 **SNAB** **Publishers Pvt Ltd**

Reprint 2006

ISBN 81-7869-072-1

Food Styling & Photography: **SNAB**

Picture on cover:	*2 Layer Tomato-Broccoli Soup*
	Crispy Spinach & Feta Salad
Picture on Page 1:	*Cream of Mushroom*
Picture on page 2-3:	*Minestrone, Chicken Pasta Salad*
Picture on page 4:	*Mulligatawny Vegetarian*
	Lotus Stem & Guava Salad
Picture on page 94:	*Orient Noodle Soup*
	Chicken Sweet Corn Soup
Picture on backcover:	*Thousand Island Tomatoes*

Layout and laser typesetting:

National Information Technology Academy
3A/3, Asaf Ali Road
New Delhi-110002
☎ 23252948

Published by:

Publishers Pvt Ltd
3A/3 Asaf Ali Road
New Delhi-110002

Editorial and Marketing office:
E-159, Greater Kailash-II, N.Delhi-48
Tel: 91-11-23250091, 23252948, Fax: 29225218
Tel: 91-11-29214011, 29218727, 29218574
E-Mail: nitamehta@email.com, nita@nitamehta.com
*Website:*http://www.nitamehta.com
Website: http://www.snabindia.com

Printed at:

BRIJBASI ART PRESS LTD.

Distributed by:

THE VARIETY BOOK DEPOT
A.V.G. Bhavan, M 3 Con Circus
New Delhi - 110 001
Tel: 23417175, 23412567; Fax: 23415335

Price: Rs. 195/-

Introduction

Soups are heart warmers which cheer you up. A good soup should be pleasing and natural without any artificial colours and free from greasiness. The flavour should be full and good, not overpowering. Too much garlic or spices should be avoided. Soups can be coveniently categorized as light and substantial.

Light soups are generally served as appetizers before the main course. Such soups should be deliciously light which make the guest look forward to dinner, being truly an appetizer! Appetizer soups if heavy, kill the appetite. Sometimes a soup may be a meal in itself. Such hearty or substantial soups, with a sandwich or some toasted bread are filling enough to make a complete meal. Substantial soups are good for family meals. After a heavy lunch, they make an ideal dinner. They are also a welcome change from the routine dal- subzi! For the calorie conscious, soups - substantial as well as light, both are good. Substantial soups should be served in a bowl with a soup spoon as it is difficult to have them straight from the cup. Substantial soups are best enjoyed at a sit-down meal, with the soup placed on the dinning table. Ofcourse that is ones own preference, but I enjoy a substantial soup when I am comfortably seated.

Soups may be very thin and clear, like the Tom Yum Thai soup, or slightly thickened by using cornflour as in Chinese soups or the vegetable itself is pureed to give the desired consistency, as in mushroom soup. There are Indian soups/shorbas like rasam, classic Continental soups like cream of tomato or cream of vegetable and other International soups like minestrone of Italy or the French onion soup of France. The semi thick soups are also called broths. The thick soups include Mulligatawny soup topped with some boiled rice.

Salads can be served as an appetizer, a dinner accompaniment or as a main course. Salads should be crisp, colourful, refreshing and delicious. There are no hard and fast rules about the ingredients that should go into a salad. Select salad ingredients to lend colour to the table, but above all let them blend and help to balance the rest of the menu. Salads are not just diet dishes - vegetables can be combined with a portion of proteins such as cheese, sprouts, egg, fish, chicken etc. The nutritive value of salads is as varied as the foods that go into it. They are a source of minerals, vitamins and fibre.

Enjoy your meal starting with a delicious and healthy salad and follow it with a steaming hot bowl of appetizing soup!

Nita Mehta

About The Recipes

What's In A Cup?

INDIAN CUP
1 teacup = 200 ml liquid
AMERICAN CUP
1 cup = 240 ml liquid (8 oz)
The recipes in this book were tested with the Indian teacup which holds 200 ml liquid.

Contents

Light Appetizer Soups   13

Substantial & Hearty Soups   38

Pasta, Rice & Noodle Salads   84

Basic Recipes   89

Glossary of Hindi to English Terms   91

Soup Accompaniments

Accompaniments are served separately or on the side in the soup plate. I prefer to serve even croutons separately, as they usually turn soggy by the time one actually starts with the soup! Ready made soup sticks can be made to look more interesting if warmed and served in a tall glass. To warm them, heat in the oven for 5 minutes.

Garlic Bread Fingers - Take a broad french loaf, cut into half lengthwise. Mix 3 tbsp softened butter with ½ tsp garlic paste, ¾ tsp each of red chilli flakes and oregano. Spread the butter on the cut surface. Cut into ¾" thick fingers. Bake them in an oven at 200°C for 12-15 minutes on the wire rack, till golden and crisp.

Spicy Nachos - Knead 1½ cups maize flour (makki ka atta) and 1 cup flour (maida) with 1 tsp salt, 1 tsp oregano, ½ tsp red chilli flakes and 2 tbsp oil, with enough water to a slightly firm dough. Make marble sized balls and roll out into thin chappatis. Prick it with a fork. Cut into 4 or 8 triangles and deep fry on medium flame till golden. Serve hot. You can make them in advance and store in an air tight container after they cool down.

Cheese Munchys - Take a bread slice and butter both sides of the bread lightly. Top with a cheese slice. Sprinkle 1 tsp of finely chopped capsicum and 1 tsp of finely chopped deseeded tomato. Sprinkle a pinch of freshly crushed pepper and salt. Place on the wire rack of a preheated oven at 200°C for 5-7 minutes, till the bread turns crisp from below. Remove from oven and cut into 4 fingers with a pizza cutter. If you like, cut each finger into half to give 8 small pieces.

Herbed Croutons - Cut 1 day old bread into tiny cubes, about ¼" cubes. Heat oil in a kadhai. Reduce heat. Add bread cubes to the hot oil and remove from oil immediately when they start to change colour, within 1 minute or they will turn extra brown. Immediately sprinkle the hot fried croutons with ¼ tsp pepper or oregano or basil or mixed herbs and a pinch of salt.

Nutty Spread - Toast 1 tsp sesame seeds (til) and 1 tsp chopped walnuts on a tawa on low heat till sesame seeds turn golden. Remove from tawa. Mix 1 tbsp softened butter with 1 tbsp cheese spread. Add toasted sesame seeds and walnuts to it. Add 1-2 tbsp milk to make the spread softer, if it is cold weather. Keep aside till serving time. At serving time, serve cold spread with warm soup sticks.

Soup Garnishes

All garnishes should be done on the soup after it has been heated and put in the soup bowl or cup, just before serving.

- Drop cream on the soup in a circle with a spoon, slowly to get a round swirl
- Grate cheese into thin long shavings on the soup
- Thinly sliced almonds add the crunch as well as eye appeal
- Very tiny pieces of paneer or capsicum or carrot (diced vegetables)
- Finely chopped greens of a spring onion or coriander or parsley
- Fried Rice noodles - these extremely thin noodles resemble long, translucent white hair. When deep fried they explode dramatically into a tangle of airy, crunchy strands that are used for garnishing soups.

Quick Stock

Seasoning Cubes (Extra Taste)

A good stock is important for most soups. However, if you do not have fresh stock ready or feel lazy to make a stock, you can use seasoning cubes mixed in water instead. Seasoning cubes are available as small packets. These are very salty, so taste the soup after adding the cube before you put more salt. Always crush the seasoning cube to a powder before using it. Vegetarian as well as chicken seasoning cubes are available.

Light Appetizer SOUPS

These are ideal for serving at parties as appetizers before the main meal. They are light and nutritive and so can be enjoyed, without disturbing the dinner.

Green Pea Soup

Serves 4

1¼ cups shelled peas (matar), 1 tbsp butter
2-3 flakes garlic - crushed, 1 onion - chopped
½ cup milk, salt & pepper to taste, a pinch sugar

1. Heat butter in a pressure cooker. Add garlic and onions. Cook till onions turn transparent.
2. Add all the peas. Saute for 2-3 minutes on low flame.
3. Add 4 cups of water. Give 3-4 whistles. Remove from fire.
4. After it cools down, take out 2 tbsp peas and keep aside for topping. Blend the remaining soup along with peas in a mixer to a smooth puree.
5. Strain the soup through a big sieve (chhanni).
5. Add milk to the strained soup. Heat the soup on low heat. Add salt-pepper to taste and sugar. Boil for 2 minutes.
6. To serve, boil soup, keeping flame low. Pour in soup bowls. Top each bowl with 5-6 cooked peas kept aside. Serve hot.

Lemon Coriander Soup

Serves 4

CLEAR STOCK
5 cups water
1 stick lemon grass - chopped or rind of 1 lemon (1 tsp rind)
¼ cup chopped coriander alongwith stalks
1" piece of ginger - washed, sliced without peeling
2 laung (cloves), 1 tej patta (bay leaf)
2 seasoning cubes (maggi or knorr or any other brand), preferably lemon flavoured

OTHER INGREDIENTS
1 tsp oil, a pinch of red chilli powder
½ carrot, 2 mushrooms
2 baby corns - cut into paper thin slices
salt & pepper to taste
2-3 tbsp lemon juice, ¼ tsp sugar
1½ tbsp cornflour dissolved in ¼ cup water
2 tbsp coriander leaves - torn roughly with the hands

1. If using lemon rind, wash and grate 1 lemon with the peel gently on the grater to get lemon rind. Do not apply pressure and see that the white pith beneath the lemon peel is not grated along with the yellow rind. The white pith is bitter!
2. Cut mushrooms into thin slices (¼ cup). Cut carrot into paper thin slices diagonally (¼ cup).
3. For stock, mix all ingredients given under clear stock with 5 cups of water. Bring to a boil. Keep on low flame for 5 minutes. Keep aside.
4. Heat 1 tsp oil in a pan. Remove from fire. Add a pinch of red chilli powder.
5. Immediately, add carrot, mushrooms and baby corns cut into paper thin slices. Return to fire. Add pepper. Saute for 1 minute on medium flame.
6. Strain the prepared stock into the vegetables in the pan. Boil. Check salt and add more if required.
7. Add 1½ tbsp cornflour dissolved in ¼ cup water, stirring continuously. Boil.
8. Add lemon juice, sugar and coriander leaves. Simmer for 1-2 minutes. Add more lemon juice if required. Remove from fire. Serve hot in soup bowls.

Carrot Soup

Serves 4

250 gm carrots - chopped very finely (2 cups)
2 tbsp butter
1 bay leaf (tej patta)
½ tsp salt or to taste, 1 tsp pepper, or to taste
2 stock cubes (maggi or knorr) dissolved in 3 cups of water to get stock
croutons of 1-2 bread slices, see page 11

1. Heat 2 tbsp butter in a pan, add chopped carrots & bay leaf. Cook for 4-5 minutes. Add salt and pepper.
2. Add 1 cup of prepared stock (cube+water). Bring to a boil and simmer for 2 minutes. Remove from fire, cool.
3. Churn in a mixer to a puree. Reheat soup and add the remaining stock (2 cups) and give 1 boil. Serve hot garnished with croutons.

Hari Moong ka Shorba

A very light delicious soup which makes a good start to an Indian meal.

Serves 4-6

1 cup green saboot moong dal - soak for ½ hour
1½ tbsp jaggery powder (gur)
¼ tsp haldi, 1½ tsp salt, 2 tbsp lemon juice
3-4 tbsp coriander - chopped

COLLECT TOGETHER
¼ tsp hing (asafoetida), ½ tsp jeera (cumin seeds), ½ tsp rai (mustard seeds)
3-4 laung (cloves), 1" stick dalchini (cinnamon)
3-4 saboot kali mirch (peppercorns), 8-10 curry leaves

GRIND TO A PASTE (1½ tsp), YOU CAN GRIND EXTRA & STORE IN THE FRIDGE
½" piece ginger, ½ green chilli, 3-4 flakes garlic

1. Soak dal for ½ hour. Drain water from the soaked dal. Add 10 cups water and salt. Cook covered for about ½ hour till the dal is done. Do not pressure cook.
2. Heat 2 tbsp oil in a heavy bottom deep pan. Add all the collected ingredients together - hing, jeera, rai, dalchini, laung, peppercorns and curry patta. Stir.
3. Add 1½ tbsp of the prepared ginger-garlic-green chilli paste. Stir.
4. Strain the water of the dal into the pan. Do not mash the dal at all.
5. Add jaggery, haldi and salt to taste. Simmer for 2 minutes.
6. Add lemon juice and coriander. Serve hot.

Cream of Tomato

The evergreen soup now made more delicious!

Serves 4

½ kg (6) ripe red tomatoes - chopped roughly
1 small onion - chopped roughly
1 carrot - chopped roughly
1 small potato - chopped roughly
1 tsp butter
1" stick cinnamon (dalchini)
4-5 saboot kali mirch (pepper corns)
3-4 laung (cloves)
1 tsp sugar
4 tbsp thick cream
salt and pepper to taste

TO SERVE
some herbed croutons, see page 11

1. Melt 1 tsp butter in a pressure cooker, add dalchini, saboot kali mirch and laung. Stir for 30 seconds.
2. Add chopped onion, carrot and potato. Stir till potato starts to change colour.
3. Add the chopped tomatoes and cook for 2-3 minutes.
4. Add 4 cups of water. Close the pressure cooker and pressure cook to give 2 whistles. Keep on low heat for 3 minutes. Remove from heat and cool.
5. Blend the cooled mixture in a mixer to a smooth puree. Strain through a sieve (chhanni) to get a smooth soup.
6. Reheat soup in a saucepan. Check salt, sugar and pepper. Add more if required.
7. Add cream to the soup. Serve hot garnished with croutons.

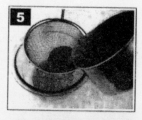

Bread Croutons

Vegetable Cheese Broth
with Cheese Balls
Serves 4-5

1 tbsp butter, 1 bay leaf (tej patta)
½ cup finely chopped cauliflower (phool gobhi)
½ cup finely chopped carrot (gajar)
½ cup finely chopped cabbage (bandgobhi)
3-4 french beans - finely chopped
¾ cup milk
3 tbsp level cornflour dissolved in ¼ cup cold milk or water
1½ tsp salt, ½ tsp pepper, ½ tsp oregano
2 tbsp finely chopped capsicum
10-15 leaves of fresh basil or tender tulsi leaves - finely shredded into thin long pieces
4 cubes cheese, (cheddar cheese) - grated (¾ cup)

CHEESE BALLS
½ cup grated paneer, 3 tbsp dry bread crumbs
¼ tsp pepper, ¼ tsp oregano, ¼ tsp salt
1 tbsp finely chopped coriander or parsley

1. Mix all ingredients of cheese balls nicely in a bowl. Make about 8-10 small balls, almost resembling the size of a marble. Keep in the fridge till serving time.
2. Heat butter in a sauce pan or kadhai, add bay leaf, cauliflower, carrot, cabbage and beans. Saute for 2-3 minutes.
3. Add 5 cups of water and bring to a boil. Cover and simmer for about 2-3 minutes, till the vegetables are slightly tender.
4. Add milk, dissolved cornflour, salt, pepper, oregano and capsicum. Give 1 boil, check the seasoning.
5. To serve, warm the cheese balls for 1 minute in a microwave or saute in a non-stick frying pan for 2 minutes in 1 tsp butter. Keep aside.
6. Put the soup on fire. Add basil. Cook 1- 2 minutes. Remove soup from fire. Add grated cheese and mix.
7. Pour hot soup in indiviual bowls, top each with 2 cheese balls and sprinkle with freshly ground pepper. If you like, you can serve the warmed cheese balls on the side, in the soup plate.

Chicken Sweet Corn Soup

Picture on page 94   *Serves 6*

200 gm chicken with bones - cut into 3-4 pieces
1 tin sweet corn (cream style, 460 gm) (2½ cups)
1 spring onion - chopped alongwith the greens, keep greens separate
2 tbsp green chilli sauce
1 tbsp red chill sauce
1 tbsp vinegar
½ tsp ajinomoto (optional)
1 tsp salt, ¼ tsp pepper or to taste
4 tbsp cornflour
2 eggs - beaten lightly

1. Put 9 cups water, chicken and 1 tsp salt in a pressure cooker. Pressure cook for 2 whistles and cook on low heat for another 2- 3 minutes. Remove from fire. Let the pressure drop by itself. Pick up the chicken pieces from the stock with the help of tongs (chimta). Let the stock remain in the cooker. Debone the meat from the chicken. Keep water (stock) in the pressure cooker aside.
2. Heat 2 tbsp oil separately in a pan. Add white of onions and chicken shreds and stir fry for 1 minute. Remove from fire.
3. Put the stock in the pressure cooker on fire, add sweet corn to stock and allow to boil on high heat for 5-7 minutes.
4. Add stir fried chicken to the simmering soup.
4. Add green chilli sauce, red chilli sauce, vinegar, ajinomoto, salt, pepper and green of spring onions to the soup in the cooker. Simmer for 1 minute.
5. Mix cornflour in ½ cup water, add to soup stirring constantly until soup is thick.
6. Beat eggs in a small bowl with a fork. Add the beaten eggs gradually, stir soup immediately with a fork in the other hand, so that threads are formed.
7. Remove from fire. Serve hot in indiviual soup bowls along with soya sauce and green chillies in vinegar.

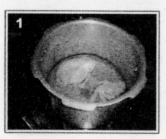

Useful Tip

If the whole tin of sweet corn is not used, store the remaining in a plastic or steel box in the freezer compartment of the refrigerator for a month or even more.

Sweet Corn Vegetable Soup

Serves 6

1 cream style sweet corn tin (460 gm), about 2½ cups
¼ cup finely chopped carrot
¼ cup finely chopped cabbage
1 spring onion - finely chopped alongwith the greens
2-3 french beans - finely chopped
2 tbsp green chilli sauce
1 tbsp red chill sauce
1 tbsp vinegar
¼ tsp pepper
2 tsp level salt
a pinch of ajinomoto
5 tbsp cornflour dissolved in ¾ cup water

1. Mix cream style corn with 9 cups water in a deep pan. Bring to a boil. Boil for 5 minutes.
2. Add chilli sauces and vinegar. Simmer for 1-2 minutes.
3. Meanwhile heat 1 tbsp oil in a nonstick pan add the vegetables. Saute for 1 minute. Add the sauteed vegetables to the simmering soup. Simmer for 1 minute.
4. Add salt, pepper and ajinomoto to the soup.
5. Add cornflour paste and cook for 2-3 minutes till the soup thickens. Serve hot.

Sweet Corn Soup with Fresh Corn

Grate 4 large corn-on-cobs (saboot bhutte), about 1 kg, keeping aside ¼ cup of whole corn kernels without grating them. Pressure cook grated and whole corn kernels with 10 cups water and 1½ tbsp sugar to give 2 whistles. Keep on low heat for 10 minutes. Continue from step 2.

Basil Tomato Soup

Sweet basil is used to flavour this tomato soup. This basil is different from the holy basil, "Tulsi", which has a hint of bitterness. However, both the basil plants - sweet basil and the holy basil belong to the same family and can be substituted.

Picture on facing page   *Serves 4*

250 gms bright red tomatoes (without any yellow patches near the stem end)
½ cup chopped fresh sweet basil leaves or ¼ cup chopped tulsi leaves
1 medium onion
1 celery stalk - chopped (2- 3 tbsp)
1 tsp chopped garlic
1 tbsp olive oil or any cooking oil
1¼ tsp salt, ½ tsp black pepper, ½ tsp orgeano, ¼ tsp sugar
2½ cups readymade coconut milk
2 tbsp readymade tomato puree
finely chopped greens of 1 spring onion (hara pyaz)

1. Cut each tomato into 4 pieces & onion into 8 pieces.
2. Chop the celery stem as shown (only stem is used).
3. Place tomatoes, onion, chopped celery stem, garlic & oil in a pan. Cover & cook over low heat for 15-20 minutes, stirring in between. Remove from fire. Add ½ cup water, salt, pepper, orgeano and sugar. Cool. Keep aside.
4. Put cooled mixture in a mixer & churn till smooth.
5. Strain through a strainer (chhanni) pressing with the back of a spoon. Put the mixture in the same pan and keep on fire.
6. Add 2½ cups coconut milk, basil and tomato puree and bring to a boil. Reduce heat.
7. Add greens of spring onion. Remove from fire. Serve hot in indiviual soup bowls.

Note: In absence of sweet basil you can use half the amount of tender tulsi leaves or coriander leaves.

Thai Green Mango Salad : Recipe on page 54, Basil Tomato Soup ➤

Lettuce Soup

Serves 4   *Picture on opposite page*

A lovely pale green, light textured soup. Surplus lettuce which is not crisp enough for salads can be utilized in a good way!

200-250 gms ice berg lettuce (1 head)
1½ tbsp butter
1 small onion - chopped
¼ tsp black pepper, ½ tsp sugar
¼ tsp grated nutmeg (jaiphal)
1 cup milk

1. Separate the lettuce leaves and wash them very well in 2-3 changes of water. Cut them into shreds. Boil 3 cups water with 1 tsp salt. Add the lettuce leaves to the boiling water and cook for 3-5 minutes in salted water. Strain. Keep stock and leaves aside separately.
2. Melt butter in a deep pan or kadhai. Cook the onion till soft, for 1-2 minutes. Keeping aside 2 tbsp lettuce shreds, add the rest to the onion. Stir.
3. Add the stock and bring to a boil. Add pepper, sugar and nutmeg. Add salt according to taste. Simmer for 1-2 minutes. Remove from fire.
4. Cool the mixture and blend it in a liquidizer. Strain the soup.
5. Add milk to the soup. Bring to a boil, stirring, and simmer for 1-2 minutes. Serve hot garnished with reserved lettuce shreds.

◁ *Red Bean & Chickpea Salad : Recipe on page 60, Lettuce Soup*

Hot & Sour

The popular Chinese soup. An all time favourite! For the non vegetarians, boil 200 gm chicken with bones in 6 cups water till chicken turns tender, about 7-8 minutes. Use the chicken liquid instead of water in the recipe. Debone boiled chicken and shred into small pieces and use it along with the vegetables. You can omit the mushrooms.

Serves 4-5

CHILLI-GARLIC PASTE
**3 dry red chillies - deseeded and soaked in water for 10 minutes
2 flakes garlic, 1 tsp vinegar, 1 tbsp oil, 2 tbsp water**

OTHER INGREDIENTS
**2 tbsp oil, 1-2 tender french beans - sliced very finely (3-4 tbsp)
1-2 tbsp dried mushrooms or 2-3 fresh mushrooms - chopped
½ cup chopped cabbage, ½ cup thickly grated carrot
6 cups water
2 vegetable seasoning cubes (maggi) - powdered, see page 12
1 tsp sugar, 1 tsp salt, ½ tsp pepper powder, or to taste
1½- 2 tbsp soya sauce, 1½ tbsp vinegar
6 tbsp cornflour mixed with ½ cup water**

1. Soak dry, red chillies in a little water for 10 minutes.
2. For the chilli-garlic paste, drain the red chillies. Grind red chillies, garlic and vinegar roughly with 2 tbsp water in a small coffee or spice grinder.
3. If dried mushrooms are available, soak them in water for ½ hour to soften. Wash thoroughly to clean the dirt in them. Cut away any hard portion and then cut into smaller pieces.
4. Heat 2 tbsp oil. Add beans and mushrooms. Stir fry for 1-2 minutes on high flame. Add cabbage and carrots. Stir for a few seconds.
5. Add the water and the seasoning cubes. Add chilli-garlic paste, sugar, salt, pepper, soya sauce and vinegar. Boil for 2 minutes.
6. Add cornflour paste, stirring continuously. Cook for 2-3 minutes till the soup turns thick. Serve hot.

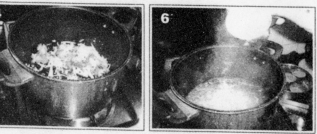

Burnt Corn Soup

Serves 2-3   *Picture on page 39*

1 big corn on the cob (bhutta), about 250-275 gms
1 green capsicum - washed
2 vegetable seasoning cubes (Maggi or Knorr), see page 12
½ tsp salt
2-3 tbsp butter or olive oil, ½ onion - finely chopped
¼ tsp finely chopped garlic
1 tsp finely chopped coriander leaves
1 tsp lemon juice

1. Roast whole corn on a naked flame, turning sides, constantly till brown specks appear on all the sides.
2. Remove from fire. Scrape roasted corn niblets with the help of a knife from the cob. Keep aside 2 tbsp corn for garnishing.
3. Pierce a fork or a knife in the capsicum and roast it on an open flame till it becomes black from various sides. Chop capsicum finely into very small pieces.
4. Crush stock cubes. Mix with 1½ cups of warm water and keep aside the stock.
5. Heat butter or oil in a saucepan or any deep pan. Add chopped onion and cook till onions turn soft. Cook for 3-4 minutes on medium flame.
6. Add garlic & roasted corn niblets. Cook for 2 minutes.
7. Add prepared stock, capsicum and salt. Give one boil.
8. Lower heat. Cook covered for 5 minutes. Remove from fire & cool. Blend coarsely in mixer to a rough paste.
9. Put this paste in the saucepan. Return to fire. Add 1½ cups of water, coriander and lemon juice. Mix well. Give one boil. Simmer for a minute.
10. Remove from fire. Serve garnished with corn niblets.

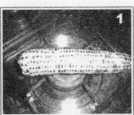

Capsicum & Cilantro Soup

A cheesy light green soup. Cilantro is another name for fresh coriander. Addition of cheese spread makes all the difference.

Serves 4

**4 medium sized capsicums - cut into big pieces, roughly chopped
2 tomatoes - cut into big pieces, 2 tbsp chopped coriander or cilantro
2 cups water, ½ cup cold milk
2 tsp cheese spread or 2 tbsp grated cheddar cheese (use tin or cubes)
1 tsp salt, ½ tsp pepper or to taste, 1 tsp butter**

1. Boil chopped capsicum and tomato pieces with 1 cup water in a saucepan (patila). Simmer for 2 minutes. Remove from the fire, cool.
2. Churn in a mixer to get a smooth puree. Add 1 cup water mix well. Strain puree.
3. Let the puree cool down completely. To the cooled puree add milk, cheese spread, salt, pepper, cilantro and butter. Keep aside till serving time. To serve, keep on low fire and heat, stirring continuously. Remove from fire when it starts to boil. Do not boil.
4. Pour into individual bowls or cups and serve hot.

Almond & Grape Soup

Serves 3

**20-25 almonds - soaked for 2-3 hours and peeled (blanched)
½ cup grapes (green), 1 tbsp butter
1 onion - chopped finely, 2 tbsp celery stalks - chopped
2-3 laung (cloves), 2-3 saboot kali mirch (peppercorns)
1 tbsp maida, 1 small carrot - chopped
1 cup milk, ½ tsp salt, ¼ tsp white pepper**

1. Place the grapes and almonds in a grinder & grind to a smooth puree. Keep aside.
2. Heat 1 tbsp butter in a deep pan, add onion, celery, laung and saboot kali mirch. Stir on low heat for 2 minutes.
3. Add maida and cook for 1 minute on low heat.
4. Add carrot and 4 cups of water. Bring to a boil, cover and simmer for 5 minutes. Remove from heat and cool. Grind it in a mixer till smooth. Strain the stock.
5. Place the strained stock in the pan. Add grape-almond mixture and milk.
6. Bring to a boil. Add salt and pepper. Check the seasoning.
7. Serve hot garnished with some chopped almonds, grapes and cream.

Everyday Vegetable Soup

Serves 4

A delicious and healthy peachish coloured soup.

1 onion - chopped roughly
2 carrots - chopped (1 cup)
1 large potato - roughly chopped or 1 large turnip (shalgam) - roughly chopped or 1 cup chopped lauki (bottle gourd)
½ cup cabbage - roughly chopped
2 tomatoes - chopped (1 cup)
2 bay leaves (tej pata), 2 laung (cloves)
¾ cup milk
1 tsp salt and ½ pepper, or to taste

1. Place carrots, onion, potato or turnip or lauki , cabbage, tomatoes, bay leaves and laung in a pressure cooker with 4 cups water. Pressure cook to give 2 whistles. Simmer on low heat for 5 minutes. Remove from fire.
2. Cool and puree the soup in a mixer or a food processor. Strain the soup.
3. Put the pureed soup back on fire. Add ¾ cup milk to the soup. Stir continuously till boils. Reduce heat.
4. Add salt and pepper. Simmer for 2-3 minutes on low heat. Serve hot.

Note: You can add 1 tsp butter to the soup at step 4 for a richer taste.

French Onion Soup

Serves 4

3 tbsp butter
2 onions - sliced very finely
4 flakes garlic - crushed
1½ tbsp flour (maida)
salt to taste, black pepper powder to taste
4 cups stock (given below) or 4 cups water mixed with 2 seasoning cubes, Page 12

STOCK
1 carrot - chopped roughly, 1 onion - chopped roughly
2 bay leaves (tej patta)
6-7 peppercorns (saboot kali mirch)
4 cups water

GARNISHING
25 gm cheddar cheese - grated (use tin or cubes)
½ tsp mustard powder
2 garlic bread slices - toasted or 1 slice of bread - toasted

1. To prepare the stock, pressure cook all ingredients of the stock with 4 cups water to give 3-4 whistles. Strain through a sieve. Keep the clear stock aside.

2. Heat butter in a clean, heavy bottomed pan or kadhai. Fry the onions and garlic over a moderately low heat, stirring occasionally to prevent sticking, until well browned. Do not let the onions burn.

3. Add the maida and cook for 1 minute on low flame.

4. Add the stock gradually, stirring continuously. Boil.

5. Add salt and pepper, and simmer for 5 minutes. Keep soup aside.

6. To garnish the soup, mix the mustard powder and cheese together in a small bowl. Spread over the toasted garlic bread slices or regular bread. Place the toasted slices in the hot oven for 2-3 minutes. Cut each garlic bread into 2 pieces or regular bread into 4 squares.

7. Serve steaming hot soup with one piece of cheese toast floating on top in each serving.

Note: To make this soup for non-vegetarians, use chicken stock (p. 89) in place of veg stock.

Orient Noodle Soup

A spicy, hot, clear soup with lots of vegetables for the winter months. Lemon rind and tomato puree add a delicious flavour to this appetizer soup. Noodles make it different.

Serves 4   *Picture on page 94*

1½ tbsp oil
3 flakes garlic - chopped & crushed
4 mushrooms - sliced and then cut into thin long pieces
1 small carrot - grated, ½ capsicum - finely chopped
10-12 spinach leaves - shredded finely (cut into thin strips)
3 tbsp readymade tomato puree
2 whole, dried red chillies - deseed & cut into small pieces with a knife
30 gms noodles (½ cup) - break into 2" pieces
1¼ tsp salt, ¼ tsp pepper
rind of 1 lemon (1 tsp approx.), see step 1
2 tsp green chilli sauce
1½ tbsp vinegar

1. To take out lemon rind, grate a firm whole lemon on the medium holes of the grater without applying too much pressure. Grate only the upper yellow skin without grating the white bitter pith beneath the yellow skin. Keep rind aside.
2. Heat oil in a pan. Reduce heat and add garlic. Saute briefly for ½ minute.
3. Add mushrooms, carrot and capsicum. Stir fry for 1 minute.
4. Add tomato puree and red chillies. Stir for ½ minute.
5. Add 4 cups of water. Bring the soup to a boil. Add the noodles. Boil on medium heat for 2-3 minutes till noodles are soft.
6. Add salt, pepper, lemon rind, chilli sauce and vinegar.
7. Add the finely shredded spinach, simmer for 1 minute. Serve hot in soup bowls.

Yakhani Murg Shorba

A clear fennel flavoured Kashmiri shorba with crisp fried onions.

Serves 8

1 (700-800 gm) chicken - cut into 8-10 pieces
4 tbsp crisp fried onions
or
2 onions - sliced thinly and deep fried crisp till golden brown
1 tbsp butter (melted)
3 tbsp chopped coriander

GROUND MASALA PASTE
10 saboot kali mirch (black pepper corns)
1 onion - finely chopped
6 flakes garlic
2 tsp saboot dhania (coriander seeds)
2" dalchini (cinnamon)
1 tsp saunf (fennel seeds), 1 tsp salt or to taste

1. Place the chicken pieces in a pressure cooker with 8 cups of water and the ground masala paste. Pressure cook to give 2 whistles and simmer for 5 minutes. Remove from heat.
2. Strain the soup in a soup strainer to get a clear stock or soup. Pick up the chicken pieces.
3. Separate the chicken pieces from the bones into small chicken shreds and keep aside.
4. Deep fry onion slices to a golden colour. Keep aside till serving time.
5. Add salt to taste, chicken shreds, chopped coriander leaves and melted butter to the clear chicken soup. Mix well.
6. At serving time, boil soup and add the fried onions Bring to a boil and pour soup in individual bowls.

Cream of Mushroom

Most of the mushrooms are pureed to give taste and texture to the soup but some are finely chopped and added towards the end for that special bite. Garnished with some greens, this soup is a treat for the mushroom lovers.

Serves 4-5   *Picture on page 1*

200 gm mushrooms
2 tsp butter
1 onion - chopped
2 flakes garlic, 1 bay leaf (tej patta)
2 tbsp maida (plain flour)
1 tsp salt, ½ tsp white pepper
1½ cups milk

TOPPING
2 tbsp cream, some chopped spring onion greens (optional)

1. Roughly chop 150 gm of mushrooms. Finely cut the remaining 50 gm of mushrooms for topping and keep aside.

2. Melt butter in a heavy bottom pan. Add chopped onion, 150 gm roughly chopped mushrooms, garlic and bay leaf. Stir for 3-4 minutes. Do not brown the onions.

3. Add maida and stir for 1 minute. Add 3 cups of water, 1 tsp salt, ½ tsp pepper and bring to a boil. Reduce heat and cook covered for 5 minutes. Remove from heat. Cool.

4. Place mixture in mixer/food processor and grind to a smooth puree. Strain puree through a soup strainer.

5. Put the puree back in the pan. Add milk and finely chopped mushrooms. Boil. Simmer for 2 minutes.

6. Lower heat and add cream and chopped spring onion greens. Mix well and serve hot.

Mushroom & Celery Soup

For Mushroom & Celery Soup, to the above mushroom soup, add 4 tbsp chopped celery stalks at step 2 along with the onion. Proceed in the same way as given above.

Tom Yum

A clear lemon flavoured Thai soup with paper thin slices of vegetables. Prawns can be added for the non vegetarian flavour instead of the vegetables. Cook prawns only for a very short time, just until they turn opaque. Even slight overcooking will harden them.

Serves 4

PASTE
2 dry red chillies, 2-3 flakes garlic, 2 tbsp oil, ½ onion - chopped, ½ tsp salt

OTHER INGREDIENTS
5 cups water
1" piece ginger - chopped finely or cut into paper thin slices
3-4 kaffir lime leaves (nimbu ke patte)
1 stalk lemon grass - cut into thin slices diagonally, see below
3- 4 mushrooms - cut into paper thin slices
1 small carrot - cut into paper thin diagonal slices
2 fresh red chillies - sliced diagonally and deseeded
2 tbsp chopped coriander leaves
juice of 1 lemon

1. Cut mushrooms and carrots into paper thin slices.
2. Prepare a paste by grinding all the ingredients of the paste in a mixer.
3. In a deep pan put water, sliced ginger, lime or lemon leaves and lemon grass. Add the above red chilli paste also to the water. After the boil, keep covered on low heat for 5 minutes.
4. Add mushrooms, carrots, red chillies and coriander. Boil for 2 minutes on medium flame.
5. Reduce heat. Add lemon juice and salt to taste. Simmer for 1 minute. Pour into individual bowls and serve hot.

About Lemon Grass

Only the light green stem of lemon grass is edible. The upper grass like portion has a lot of flavour but is not edible. So to use lemon grass, remove the grass portion. Discard 1" hard portion from the base of the stalk of lemon grass and then cut the stalk into thin slices. Tie the remaining grass portion into a knot. You can put this flavourful knot in soups and discard it at serving time.

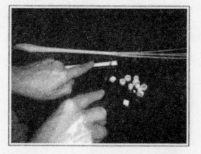

Tibetan Mince Soup

Serves 4

200 gms chicken mince (keema)
7-8 mushrooms - sliced, ¼ cup boiled rice
4 spring onions - sliced thinly including the greens
1 tsp pepper (kali mirch), 1 tsp salt, or to taste

STOCK
4 cups water mixed with 2 chicken seasoning cubes (maggi or knorr), Page 12

1. Heat 4 tbsp oil in a pan. Add chopped onion including the greens, cook till soft.
2. Add chicken mince and stir fry for 3-4 minutes on high flame. Stir continously.
3. Add mushrooms and saute for 2 minutes on medium flame.
4. Reduce heat. Add the stock and pepper. Give 1 boil. Check taste and add salt. Simmer for 2 minutes. Keep aside till serving time.
5. At serving time, boil soup. Add boiled rice, bring to a boil. Serve hot.

Spinach & Mushroom Soup

Serves 3-4   *Picture on page 40*

1 cup roughly chopped spinach leaves
6 mushrooms - sliced very finely (paper thin slices)
2 cups milk
½ tbsp butter, 1 flake garlic - crushed
2 cups water mixed with 2 tbsp cornflour
4-6 peppercorns - crushed, 1 tsp salt, or to taste, 1 tsp lemon juice

1. Slice mushrooms into paper thin slices.
2. Boil chopped spinach with milk. Cook uncovered, for about 5 minutes or till spinach softens. Remove from fire. Cool. Strain the spinach and reserve the milk.

2. Put spinach in a blender with a little milk and roughly blend. Do not blend too much. Keep spinach puree aside.
3. Heat ½ tbsp butter. Saute a crushed flake of garlic. Add mushrooms and saute for 2 minutes. Add the spinach puree and the milk kept aside.
4. Add 2 cups water mixed with 2 tbsp cornflour. Stir till it boils. Cook stirring frequently for 3-4 minutes. Add salt and freshly crushed pepper to taste.
5. Remove from fire. To serve, boil soup. Add lemon juice. Mix gently. Serve hot.

Jade Soup

A green coloured broccoli soup. Spinach adds to the nutrition as well as the colour. Carrot and beans give the crunch.

Serves 4

1 cup chopped broccoli (hari gobhi)
1 cup chopped spinach (palak)
1½ tbsp butter
2 tbsp chopped onion
1 small potato - chopped
2 tej patta (bay leaves)
2-3 laung (cloves)
3-4 saboot kali mirch (peppercorns)
1 cup milk
2 tbsp carrots - chopped into tiny pieces
2-3 french beans - chopped into tiny pieces
1¼ tsp salt, ¼ tsp white or black pepper
¼ cup cream (optional)

TO GARNISH
2-3 almonds (badam) - chopped finely or a swirl of cream

1. Heat butter in a heavy bottom deep pan. Add chopped onion, potato, tej patta, laung and kali mirch. Saute for 3 minutes.
2. Add broccoli and spinach, cook for 2 minutes.
3. Add 4 cups of water and bring to a boil. Lower heat, cover and cook for 5 minutes. Remove from fire. Cool. Discard the bay leaf and blend in a mixer to a smooth puree. Strain puree through a sieve (chhanni).
4. To the strained soup, add milk, carrots, beans, salt and pepper. Return to fire. Reheat the strained soup. Bring to a boil, stirring continuously.
5. Reduce heat, add cream, mix well. Remove from fire. Do not cook for long, after adding cream.
6. Serve hot topped with a swirl of cream or a few chopped almonds.

Tomato Rasam

A light and spicy South Indian appetizer. Best enjoyed with papad!

Serves 4

**5-6 tomatoes - whole ·
3 cups water
¼ tsp haldi (turmeric) powder, salt to taste (1½ tsp approx.)
¼ tsp hing (asafoetida) powder
coriander leaves for garnishing**

**RASAM POWDER
5 dry, whole red chillies
3 tsp saboot dhania (coriander seeds)
¼ tsp sarson (mustard seeds)
½ tsp jeera (cumin seeds)
8-10 curry leaves
1 tsp oil**

1. Boil whole tomatoes with 1 cup of water. Keep on low flame for 10 minutes till tomatoes turn soft. Remove from fire and add the remaining (2 cups) water.

2. Mash lightly to extract juice. Strain the tomatoes through a strainer to extract juice. Discard skins and keep tomato juice aside.

3. Prepare the rasam powder by frying all the ingredients of the powder together on a tawa or in a kadhai on very low flame for 3-4 minutes, till it turns fragrant and starts to smell. Powder finely.

4. To the tomato juice, add salt and haldi. Boil.

5. Add rasam powder and hing powder. Simmer for 10 minutes.

6. Garnish with coriander leaves and serve hot with papads.

Cream of Chicken

Serves 7- 8

300 gm chicken with bones - cut into 5-6 pieces
1 bay leaf (tej patta)
4 tbsp butter, 4 tbsp maida (plain flour)
3 cups milk
1 tsp freshly ground pepper, 2½ tsp salt or to taste

TO SERVE
4 tbsp cream, some chopped parsley or coriander

1. Place the chicken pieces, bay leaf and salt in a pressure cooker with 9 cups of water, and pressure cook to give 2 whistles. Simmer for 2-3 minutes, remove and cool.
2. Pick up the chicken pieces from the stock, reserving the stock.
3. Debone the meat from the bones. Discard the bones and bay leaf.
4. Heat butter in a deep pan, add maida, and cook on low heat, till maida is slightly cooked.
5. Add milk and cook till slightly thick.
6. Add the reserved stock and freshly ground pepper and salt. Bring to a boil.
7. Add the shredded chicken, mix well. Boil. Check the seasonings.
8. Pour into individual soup bowls and serve garnished with some chopped parsley and 1 tsp of cream in each cup.

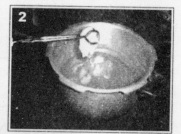

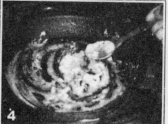
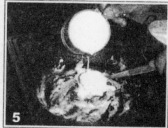

Tomato & Coriander Shorba

A thin tomato soup with the authentic Indian flavour. Coriander adds it's refreshing taste.

Serves 4

1 kg (12 medium) red tomatoes - chopped roughly
400 ml (2½ teacups) water
4 tsp besan (gram flour)
½ cup finely chopped fresh coriander
1 tbsp oil
1 tsp jeera (cumin seeds)
8-10 curry leaves
2-3 green chillies - slit lengthwise
1 tsp sugar or to taste
1 tsp salt or to taste
1 tsp lemon juice or to taste

1. Pressure cook the tomatoes with water to give one whistle. Keep on low flame for 5-7 minutes. Remove from fire.
2. When it cools down, blend in a mixer. Strain and keep tomato juice aside.
3. Add besan to 4 cups water and blend well in the mixer. Keep aside.
4. Heat oil in a pan and reduce flame. Add jeera. Let it turn golden.
5. Add curry leaves, green chillies, tomato juice, water mixed with besan and sugar. Boil.
6. Add coriander leaves and salt to taste.
7. Cook for 4-5 minutes. Add lemon juice to taste. Serve hot.

Substantial & Hearty SOUPS

These are filling soups which with a few snacks like sandwiches or soup accompaniments like soup sticks or bread sticks, make a complete meal. These hearty ones make good family soups, when the family wants to have a light dinner of soup and bread. So often when we feel like restricting the calories, a bowl of such a soup will make an excellent full meal.

These soups should be served in a bowl with a soup spoon as it is difficult to have them straight from the cup. Substantial soups are best enjoyed at a sit down meal, with the soup bowl placed on the dinning table. Ofcourse that is ones own preference, but I enjoy them when I am comfortably seated.

A good salad with a nice dressing followed by a filling soup is a welcome change from the routine dal- subzi. Serve a warm bread basket with the soup for a very satisfying meal.

Burnt Corn Soup : Recipe on page 25 ➤
Mixed Capsicum Salad : Recipe on page 52 ➤

2 Layer Tomato-Broccoli Soup

A delicious tomato soup topped with a healthy broccoli topping.

Picture on cover   *Serves 6*

1 small onion - chopped roughly
1 carrot - chopped roughly, 1 small potato - chopped roughly
½ kg (5-6) ripe red tomatoes - chopped roughly
1 tsp butter
1" stick dalchini (cinnamon), 4-5 saboot kali mirch (peppercorns), 3-4 laung (cloves)
1 tsp tomato ketchup
4 tbsp thick cream
1½ tsp salt and ½ tsp pepper or to taste

2ND LAYER (TOPPING)
½ cup chopped broccoli
¼ tsp salt, ¼ tsp pepper

1. Melt 1 tbsp butter in a pressure cooker, add dalchini, saboot kali mirch and laung. Stir for 30 seconds.
2. Add chopped onion, carrot and potato. Stir for about 3-4 minutes, till onion starts to change colour.
3. Add the chopped tomatoes and cook for 2-3 minutes.
4. Add 3 cups of water and 1 tsp salt. Cover the pressure cooker and pressure cook to give 1-2 whistles. Simmer for 3-4 minutes. Remove from heat and cool. Strain and reserve the liquid as well as the solids in the strainer.
5. Blend the solids to a smooth puree. Mix the strained liquid with the puree to get a soup.
6. Reheat the soup in a saucepan. Check salt, pepper. Add more if required. Keep aside.
7. In a separate pan heat 2 tsp butter, add chopped broccoli, saute for 2 minutes. Add ¼ tsp salt, pepper and ¾ cup water. Give one boil. Remove from fire. Cool and churn in a mixer to a smooth thick puree. Add 1 tbsp water. Keep aside.
8. To serve, separately reheat the tomato soup and the broccoli topping to a boil. Pour the prepared tomato soup in serving bowls. Swirl 2 tbsp of hot broccoli topping over the tomato soup in each bowl. Serve immediately.

◁ *Spinach & Mushroom Soup : Recipe on page 33*
◁ *Roasted Pepper & Pasta Salad : Recipe on page 86*

Minestrone

The most popular Italian soup. Use chicken for the non vegetarians (see note).

Picture on page 2   *Serves 4-5*

2 tbsp olive oil or any cooking oil
1 onion - chopped finely (½ cup), 2 flakes garlic - crushed
1 small potato - diced into very small pieces (½ cup)
1 carrot - diced into small pieces (½ cup)
3-4 tbsp finely chopped celery or green french beans
3 medium sized tomatoes - blanched, peeled and chopped finely `
2-3 tbsp baked beans, (optional) see note
salt & pepper to taste
¼ cup of macaroni or any other small pasta
5 cups stock or 5 cups water mixed with 2 seasoning cubes, see note

1. To blanch the tomatoes, put them in boiling water for 3-4 minutes. Remove from water and peel them to remove skin. Chop them finely. Keep aside.
2. Heat oil. Add onion & garlic. Stir fry till light brown.
3. Add carrots and potatoes and stir fry for 1-2 minutes.
4. Add diced chicken/macaroni. Stir for 1-2 minutes.
5. Add celery and tomatoes. Cook 2-3 minutes.
6. Add stock and baked beans.
7. Give one boil. Lower heat. Cover and simmer for 15 minutes. Add salt and pepper to taste and mix well.
8. Serve hot, garnished with some grated cheese.

Note:

- *For **chicken minestrone**, ½ cup boneless chicken (125 gm) - diced (cut into small cubes) can be used instead of macaroni. Add chicken at step 4 and stir fry for 3- 4 minutes and then proceed in the same way as written.*

- Instead of stock (made at home), 5 cups water and 2 chicken seasoning cubes can be used. Do not add any salt, if using soup cubes as they already contain salt. Taste at the end and adjust salt to taste.

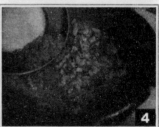

- The left over baked beans can be stored in a clean stainless steel or a plastic container in the freezer compartment of the refrigerator without getting spoilt for a month.

Pasta & Bean Soup

Serves 4

1 cup (kidney beans) rajmah, (a mixture of red and chitra rajmah) - soaked in water
overnight or for 6-8 hours
1 tbsp oil
2 spring onions - thinly sliced including the greens
1-2 garlic flakes - crushed
1 cup sliced baby corns
2 vegetable seasoning cubes - crushed, page 12
5 tbsp tiny soup pasta
3 tbsp tomato puree
4 tbsp finely chopped red capsicum or deseeded chopped tomatoes
2-3 tsp tabasco sauce, or to taste, salt and black pepper

1. Drain the beans and place in a pressure cooker with 5 cups water. After the first whistle, reduce heat and keep on low flame for 15 minutes. Do not make them too soft. Cook until nearly tender.
2. Heat the oil in a large pan and fry white part of spring onion, garlic and baby corns for 2 minutes.
3. Add the seasoning cubes and the beans with about 4 cups of their liquid.
4. Add the pasta. Cover and simmer for 10 minutes or till the pasta gets cooked.
5. Stir in the tomato puree, spring onion greens and red capsicum or tomato pieces.
6. Add tabasco sauce, salt and pepper to taste. Remove from fire. Serve hot.

Useful Tip

I always keep boiled rajmahs stored in a box in the freezer compartment of my refrigerator. They come in very handy to make soups or just for topping a piece of garlic toast with some cheese sprinkled on it. I even use them in my baked dishes.

SLICING GREEN ONIONS

DESEEDING TOMATOES

Wonton Vegetable Soup

Serves 6

WONTON WRAPPERS
1 cup plain flour (maida), ½ tsp salt, 1 tbsp oil, a little water (chilled)

WONTON FILLING
**½ of a small onion - finely chopped, ½ carrot - chopped very finely
8 french beans - chopped very finely or 1 cup chopped mushrooms
½ cup cabbage - finely chopped
a pinch of ajinomoto (optional), ½ tsp white pepper, ½ tsp sugar
1 tsp soya sauce, salt to taste**

WONTON SOUP
**6 cups vegetable stock, see page 90
2 spring onions - chopped finely alongwith the greens
1 tbsp soya sauce, 1 tsp white pepper, 1 tsp sugar, ¼ tsp ajinomoto (optional)**

1. To prepare the wonton wrappers, sift plain flour and salt.
2. Add oil and rub with finger tips till the flour resembles bread crumbs. Add chilled water gradually and make a stiff dough. Knead the dough well for about 4-5 minutes till smooth. Cover dough with a damp cloth. Keep aside for ½ hour.
3. To prepare the filling, heat 1 tbsp oil. Stir fry onions, for a few seconds.
4. Add all other vegetables. Stir fry for 1- 2 minutes. Add ajinomoto, pepper, sugar, soya sauce and salt. Mix. Remove from fire. Cool filling before making wontons.
5. Divide the dough into 4 balls. Roll out each ball into thin chappatis.
6. Cut into 2" squares. (a) Place some filling in centre. (b) Fold in half by lifting one corner & joining to the opposite corner to make a triangle. Press sides together. (c) Fold a little again, pressing firmly at both sides of the filling, but leaving corners open.

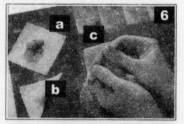

7. Bring 2 corners together, and cross over infront of the filling. Brush lightly with water where they meet, to make them stick. Keep wontons aside. (The wontons may be folded into different shapes like money bags, nurses caps or envelopes).

8. To serve the soup, boil vegetable stock, add the prepared wontons. Cover and cook for 12-15 minutes on low flame till they float on the top.
9. Add spring onions, soya sauce, pepper, sugar and ajinomoto. Simmer for 1- 2 minutes. Remove from fire. Serve hot.

Winter Mutton Broth

Serves 4-5

300 gm boneless mutton (lamb), 2½ tbsp flour (maida)
2 cups readymade coconut milk or 1 cup grated fresh coconut, see note
1 carrot - cut into small pieces
4-5 french beans - cut into small pieces
1 small potato - cut into small pieces
1 small onion - chopped into small pieces
1 green chilli - chopped into small pieces
1" piece ginger
3-4 saboot kali mirch (peppercorns)
½" dalchini (cinnamon), 2 laung (cloves)
seeds of 2 chhoti illaichi (green cardamoms) - crushed
1½ tsp salt, ¼ tsp haldi (turmeric powder)
1 tsp lemon juice

1. Wash mutton. Cut mutton pieces into tiny pieces, about ¼" pieces. Pat dry, sprinkle maida over them and mix to coat the pieces well.

3. Heat 2 tbsp oil in a pressure cooker. Add onion, green chilli, ginger, peppercorns, cinnamon, cloves and crushed seeds of green cardamom. Cook for 1-2 minutes or till onions turn transparent.

4. Add the mutton pieces and stir fry for 5-6 minutes stirring constantly (or the mutton pieces will stick at the bottom).

5. Add 1 cup of coconut milk, salt and haldi. Add 3 cups water and pressure cook to give 2 whistles. Lower the heat and simmer for 15 minutes. Remove from heat and let the pressure drop. Open the lid and check the mutton pieces, they should be absolutely tender.

6. Return to heat, add about 2 cups water and all the vegetables. Bring to a boil. Simmer for 5 minutes or till the vegetables are tender.

7. Add the remaining coconut milk and heat gently for 2-3 minutes.

8. Add lemon juice, mix. Check seasonings and add salt and pepper to taste. Remove from fire. Serve hot.

FRESH COCONUT MILK:

Extract fresh coconut milk by placing 1 cup freshly grated coconut in a mixer. Add 1 cup warm water and churn for 1 minute. Strain to get 1 cup milk. Keep milk aside. Put the coconut extract which is in the strainer, back in the blender again with 1 cup warm water. Churn & strain again to get 1 more cup coconut milk. Mix both coconut milks.

Mulligatawny Vegetarian

A lentil soup, pepped up with black pepper! Also called "pepper water".

Picture on page 4   *Serves 4-5*

¼ cup dhuli masoor dal (orange dal) - soaked for atleast 1 hour, or more
1½ tbsp butter
2 onions - chopped
2 carrots - chopped
1 small apple - peeled and chopped
1½ tbsp curry powder (MDH)
2 vegetable seasoning cubes (maggi) mixed with 5 cups water
1½ tsp salt
¾ tsp freshly crushed peppercorns (saboot kali mirch)
¼ cup boiled rice
1½ tbsp lemon juice, or to taste

GARNISH
1-2 tbsp finely chopped coriander

1. Strain water from the dal. Keep aside.
2. Heat butter in a deep pan. Add onion, carrots and apple. Stir for 3-4 minutes till onions turn very light brown.

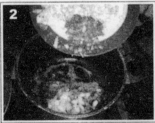

3. Add curry powder and stir for ½ minute only.
4. Add dal. Add water mixed with seasoning cubes. Boil. Cover and simmer for 20 minutes or till dal turns soft.
5. Remove from fire. Let it cool. After it cools, grind to a puree. Strain the soup through a soup sieve.
6. Put soup back on fire. Add salt and pepper. Add rice. Check salt. Cook for 2 minutes.

7. Add lemon juice and remove from fire. Serve hot in soup bowls, garnished with some chopped coriander.

Mutton Mulligatawny

Serves 4-5

350-400 gm mutton (boneless) - cut into small, ¼" pieces
2 tbsp channa dal
2 cups ready made coconut milk (available in tetra packs)
½ onion - finely chopped, 1 green chilli - chopped, 10-15 curry leaves
pinch of haldi powder (turmeric), ¼ tsp pepper
2 tbsp boiled rice

GRIND TO A PASTE
½ onion - chopped, 2 garlic flakes - chopped
½ tbsp ginger - chopped, ½ tbsp crushed pepper corns (kali mirch kuti hui)
½ tbsp jeera, ½ tbsp mustard seed (rai), ½ tbsp khus khus (poppy seeds)
½ tbsp coriander powder (dhania powder), 1 tsp salt

1. Dry roast channa dal on a tawa, on low heat for 2-3 minutes, stirring continuously, till golden brown. Keep aside.
2. Pour 1 cup coconut milk in a cooker and add mutton pieces, channa dal, ground paste and 3 cups of water. Close the lid and pressure cook to 2 whistles and simmer for 15 minutes. Remove from heat and let the pressure drop. Open the lid and check that the mutton pieces are absolutely tender. If not tender, pressure cook for another 5-7 minutes.
3. Strain the soup, reserving the liquid. Press the dal in the strainer well with a big spoon (kadcchi) while straining to ensure that channa dal strains into the soup. Keep aside the liquid and the mutton in the strainer.
4. In a deep pan, heat 2 tbsp oil. Add onion, green chilli and curry leaves and stir fry for 2-3 minutes till onions are transparent. Lower heat and add the cooked mutton pieces which are in the strainer. Stir fry mutton for 1-2 minutes.
5. Add the liquid, haldi and pepper. Bring to a boil.
6. Add the remaining coconut milk and keep on low heat. Check the seasoning and add more salt and pepper if required. Bring to a boil.
7. Serve hot in soup bowls, sprinkled with a tsp of boiled rice.

FRESH COCONUT MILK:

Extract coconut milk by placing 1 cup freshly grated coconut in a mixer. Add 1 cup warm water and churn for 1 minute. Strain to get 1 cup milk. Keep milk aside. Put the coconut extract which is in the strainer in the blender again with 1 cup more warm water. Churn & strain again to get 1 cup more of coconut milk. Mix both coconut milk.

Spiced Pumpkin Soup

Serves 6

2 tbsp butter, 1 onion - finely chopped
3 cups deseeded, peeled and cubed pumpkin (choose unripe one with greenish
skin and whitish from inside), 1 tbsp flour (maida)
a pinch of grated jaiphal (nutmeg), ½ tsp dalchini powder (ground cinnamon)
2½ cups water mixed with 1 vegetable seasoning cube to make stock
1 cup ready made orange juice
¼ tsp brown sugar (optional), ¼ tsp salt
½ tsp oregano, ½ tsp black pepper
1 tsp butter, 1½ tbsp lemon juice

TOPPING
1 tbsp magaz (melon seeds) or almonds cut into thin long pieces
1 bread slice - to make a few croutons

1. Heat 2 tbsp butter in a large deep pan, add the onion and pumpkin. Stir fry for 4-5 minutes.
2. Add maida, jaiphal and dalchini powder. Cook covered for 2 minutes, stirring occasionally.
3. Add 1 cup of stock, orange juice, brown sugar and salt. Reduce the heat and simmer for 10 minutes, until the pumpkin has softened. Remove from fire. Cool.
4. Pour the cooled mixture into a mixer and churn until smooth. Strain the soup. Return the pureed soup to the same pan.
5. Add the remaining stock, ½ cup water, oregano, pepper, 1 tsp butter, and lemon juice. Give one boil. Check salt and pepper. Keep aside.
6. To make the croutons, cut the bread into ¼" square pieces. Heat oil in a kadhai. Reduce heat. Add bread cubes and fry gently until just beginning to brown. Remove immediately from oil on a paper napkin.
7. Toast melon seeds or almonds on a tawa for 1-2 minutes, till golden and fragrant.
8. Serve the soup hot, topped with a few croutons and melon seeds or toasted almonds. Serve the remaining croutons separately.

Cheese Soup

Serves 5-6

2 tbsp oil or butter, 3 medium potatoes - peeled & chopped
2 onions - chopped
5 cups water, 1 cup milk
½ cup fresh cream mixed with 1 tsp lemon juice
2 tbsp cheese spread
1 tsp salt, ½ tsp black pepper or to taste

GARNISHING
2 toasted slices of bread
2 cubes (40 gm) cheese, fresh coriander leaves
½ tsp peppercorns (saboot kali mirch) - crushed roughly

1. Put butter or oil in a pressure cooker. Add onions and stir till light brown.
2. Add potatoes and saute for 1-2 minutes. Add 5 cups water and give 3-4 whistles to the cooker. Remove from fire.
3. When cool, strain, keeping the liquid (stock) aside. Grind the pressure cooked onion and potatoes in the strainer. Put them in a mixer/grinder and grind to a puree with about 1 cup liquid (stock) kept aside.
4. Strain the puree through a strainer. Mix with the leftover stock.
5. Boil 1 cup milk separately in a clean pan. Remove from fire.
6. Boil the soup separately. Keeping the soup on very low flame (the soup should not be boiling) add the boiled milk and cheese spread, stirring continuously. Simmer for 2-3 minutes on low flame.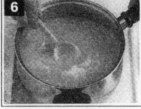
7. Add cream mixed with lemon juice, keeping the flame on very low heat and gently stirring continuously.
8. Immediately remove the soup from fire. Keep aside till serving time.
9. To serve, grate cheese on a toasted slice of bread and put it in a hot oven for 8-10 minutes till crisp from the bottom. Cut diagonally to form small triangles. Arrange a coriander leaf on each piece.
10. Heat the soup till it just starts to boil. Pour in bowls and put 1-2 pieces of cheese triangles in each serving. Serve sprinkled with freshly crushed pepper.

Salad Tips

FOR SUCCESS IN SALAD MAKING...

- Use fresh crisp ingredients.
- Wash vegetables carefully in running water if possible.
- Pat dry leafy vegetables and other vegetables on a clean kitchen towel for complete removal of moisture after washing.
- Always tear lettuce apart, never cut with a knife.
- Add colour and variety by using tomatoes, grated or diced carrots, colourful fruits and nuts.
- Be careful about the texture. Do not use too soft and mushy fruits and vegetables. If the tomatoes are soft, it is a good idea to deseed them.
- Thorough chilling is a secret to success in salad. Chill the salad bowl or plate as well as the ingredients in a refrigerator.
- Dressing should be poured at the time of serving to maintain the crispness of the greens. Toss the salad gently at the last moment. Use a large bowl and salad tongs or forks to toss the salad.
- Use of appropriate dressing makes all the difference. Dressing is the key to success. Too much dressing makes the salad limp and runny. On the other hand too little dressing makes the salad taste dry. The dressing should be just enough to coat the vegetables/meat.
- Different flavouring can be added to the dressing, like fresh herbs (mint, parsley, dill, basil); dried herbs, freshly crushed pepper, mustard and chilli flakes. Make it tangy with lemon juice and lemon rind, pickled onion and jalapenos.
- Finally, bring eye appeal. Cut your vegetable and fruits in generous chunks or slices. Simple coulourless salad can be improved by simple garnishing of crisp tomato rose or spring onion flower or fruit slices, to make your creation more interesting and attractive.

Vegetarian SALADS

Salads should be crisp, colourful, refreshing and delicious. There are no hard and fast rules about the ingredients that should go into a salad. Select salad ingredients to lend colour to the table, but above all let them blend and help to balance the rest of the menu. Salads can be served as an appetizer, a dinner accompaniment or as a main course. A frosty fruit salad can be had as a dessert too.

Ready made mayonnaise, even eggless ones are easily available today. Although the recipe for making mayonnaise is given at the end of the book, keeping a bottle of ready made one is a good idea. It has a longer shelf life than the home made one and is very handy at times. Similarly it is good to stock ready made salsa and mustard paste too. Tetra packs of fresh cream also have a longer shelf life than the fresh dairy cream. I always have a 200 gm tetra pack of fresh cream in my refrigerator.

Steamed Sesame Sticks

Taste very good as an appetizer before the main meal and also with the meal.

Serves 4

4 carrots - peeled & cut into thick match sticks (2 cups)
1 small cucumber (kheera) - cut into thick match sticks without peeling (1½ cups)
2 tbsp sesame seeds (til)

DRESSING (MIX TOGETHER WITH A WIRE WHISK)
2 tbsp olive oil, 2 tbsp vinegar
2 tbsp readymade orange juice, ½ tsp salt, ½ tsp pepper

wire whisk

colander

1. Put 4 cups of water in a pan and bring to a boil. Place a colander (a big steel strainer with big holes) on the pan. Put the carrot pieces in the colander. Cover colander with a lid and steam the carrots for 2 minutes.
2. Uncover and add the cucumber. Cover and steam further for 1 minute.
3. Remove to a bowl. Pour the dressing over the vegetable sticks and mix well. Keep covered in the fridge till serving time.
4. To serve, toast the sesame seeds on a tawa for 2 minutes on low heat till golden.
5. Pick up the vegetable sticks from the bowl and place in a flat platter. Sprinkle sesame seeds and serve.

Mixed Capsicum Salad

A very colourful and decorative salad. In the absence of coloured capsicums, use the same quantity of green capsicums.

Picture on page 39   *Serves 5*

½ cup finely chopped red capsicum
½ cup finely chopped yellow capsicum
½ cup finely chopped green capsicum
2 spring onions - finely chopped along with the green part (1 cup)
½ cup finely chopped onion
3 tbsp fresh cilantro/green coriander - finely chopped
1 tbsp finely chopped pickled jalapenos or 1 tsp chopped green chillies
¾ tsp salt
2-3 tbsp lemon juice
3 tbsp olive oil

1. Chop all ingredients very finely. Put all the ingredients of the salad in a bowl and mix well. Chill in the fridge for 1-2 hours before serving.
2. Mix well once before serving. Serve chilled with any snack or by itself.

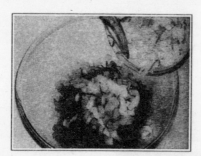 

Italian Sour Cream Salad

Serves 4　　　　　　　　Picture on page 58

SOUR CREAM DRESSING
1 cup thick curd - hang for 30 minutes in a muslin cloth
2-3 tbsp grated cheddar cheese (use tin or cubes)
75 gm (½ cup fresh cream)
2 tbsp roasted peanuts - split into halves or pounded
2 flakes garlic - crushed to a paste
1 tbsp olive oil
½ tsp oregano, 1 tsp tomato ketchup, ½ tsp salt, ¼ tsp pepper

OTHER INGREDIENTS
¾ cup carrots - cut into ¼" pieces
½ cup sliced baby corns (round slices) - paper thin slices
¼ cup chopped french beans, 2 tbsp chopped celery stalks
½ cup finely chopped cucumber or shredded capsicum
3 slices tinned pineapple - chopped into small pieces
a few lettuce leaves - torn into 1" pieces

GARNISH
some musambi or red or green capsicum rings
a tomato - to make a rose, see page 57

1. Hang curd for 30 minutes in a muslin cloth.
2. Mix all ingredients of the sour cream dressing with a wire whisk till smooth. Keep aside in the fridge.
3. Boil 4-5 cups of water with 1 tsp salt and 1 tsp sugar. Add french beans, carrots and baby corns in boiling water and cook for 1-2 minutes till crisp tender. Do not over boil.
4. When done, drain immediately and refresh by putting in cold water (so as to retain their colour). Strain. Keep in the strainer for 10 minutes.
5. Mix all vegetables and fruit in a large bowl.
6. Add the prepared dressing gradually over the fruit and vegetable mixture, mixing gently. Check salt and pepper. Transfer to a serving dish.
7. Make a border of capsicum or halved musambi slices. Make a tomato rose in the centre. Serve cold.

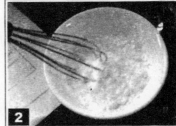

Thai Green Mango Salad

A very unusual and quick salad. Goes well with an Indian meal. It is generally eaten like a chutney, so make a small bowl for 4-6 people.

Picture on page 21   *Serves 6-8*

3 cups juliennes (match sticks) of raw green, mangoes (3 big mangoes)
½ cup roasted or fried kaju (cashew nuts) or peanuts
1-2 spring onions
OR
½ small onion and ½ capsicum - cut into shreds (thin long strips)
2-3 tbsp mango chutney (you can use home made or ready made)
1-2 dry red chillies - crushed (½ tsp)
1 tsp soya sauce, salt and pepper to taste
3-4 flakes garlic - crushed
1 tsp honey or powdered sugar, if needed

1. Cut white bulb of spring onion into rings and greens into 1" diagonal pieces.
2. Peel green mangoes. Cut the side pieces. Cut into thin match sticks or juliennes. Keep aside.
3. Mix all ingredients except cashew nuts and honey in a bowl. Add sugar or honey if mangoes are very sour. Keep covered in the refrigerator for 2-3 hours for the flavour to penetrate.
4. At serving time, top with roasted or fried nuts and mix lightly.

Note: Ready-made mango chutney is available in the market in small bottles.

Pineapple & Potato Salad

Serves 6

4 potatoes - peeled and cut into ¾" cubes
2 cups fresh ripe and yellow pineapple - chopped, (buy one which is yellow)
2 spring onions

DRESSING
1½ cups fresh curd - hang for ½ hour in a muslin cloth (mal- mal ka kapda)
¾ tsp salt, ½ tsp pepper, 1 tsp vinegar

TEMPERING/TADKA
3 tbsp olive oil, 1 tsp chopped garlic
¾ tsp rai (mustard seeds), ¾ tsp jeera (cumin seeds)
3 tbsp melon seeds (magaz) or chopped almonds

TOPPING
3 tbsp mint leaves (poodina) - chopped

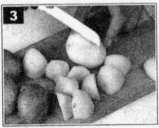

1. Hang curd in a muslin cloth for ½ hour.
2. Cut spring onions into slices up to the greens (1 cup).
3. Peel the potatoes and cut into ¾" pieces.
4. Boil 6 cups of water with 1 tsp salt. Add the potatoes and boil for about 20 minutes till tender but firm. Check with a knife to see that they are cooked.
5. Mix the potatoes with pineapple and spring onions.
6. Put the hung curd in a big bowl and add salt, pepper and vinegar. Mix well with a fork or wire whisk.
7. Add the potato- vegetable mixture to the curd. Mix well. Transfer to a serving bowl.
8. Heat olive oil in a small pan on very low heat. Add garlic, rai and jeera. Cook till jeera turns golden. Add magaz or almonds. Stir.
9. Pour this immediately over the potato salad. Chill in the fridge till serving time.
10 At the time of serving top the salad with chopped mint leaves. Serve.

SALAD GARNISHES

Carrot & Radish Tuberoses: Take a slender carrot or radish. Peel and wash it. Make a sharp angled cut, at about a height of 1½", about ½" downwards and inwards. Make 2 similar cuts from the remaining sides - all the cuts should meet at the end. Hold the top of the carrot with one hand, and the base with the other. Twist the lower portion to break off the top portion. You will have a tuberose in one hand and the remaining part of the carrot in the other. Trim the left over carrot to get a pointed end. Make more flowers from the left over carrot. Keep them in ice-cold water for upto 3-4 days without getting spoilt. You can make such flowers with white radish (mooli) also. Goes well with light French dressing salads.

Spring Onion Flowers: Cut off about ¼ inch piece from the white bulb end and leaving 3" from the bulb, cut off the greens. Slice the bulb thinly lengthwise till the end of the bulb. Now make similar cuts at right angles. Similarly for a green side, cut the green leaves almost till the stem end to get thin strips. Place in iced water for some time until it opens up like a flower. A good garnish for a Chinese salad!

Chilli Flower: Choose a slightly thick chilli. Cut into half starting from the tip almost till the end, leaving ½" from stem end. Cut each half with a scissor into many thin strips, keeping all intact at base. Put it in chilled water for 4-5 hours in the fridge. It opens up to a flower. Goes well with a spicy Thai salad!

Coloured Capsicum Baskets: Slice the top of a coloured (yellow, red or green capsicum). Make ½" deep V cuts all around the edge to get a 'VVVV' edge. Leave the bunch of seeds in it as they are. Place on the side of a large platter of salad.

Tomato Rose: Take a very firm red tomato. Beginning at stem end, start cutting the skin as though you were peeling it in a long strip. The strip should be as long as possible, as thin as possible and about ½" to 1" wide. See that you keep changing the width of the strip as you go on peeling it. Do not let the strip be uniform in width. The rose looks more natural if the strip is cut uneven. If while peeling, it breaks, keep the broken part aside for use later on and continue cutting the peel. Now start rolling up the long strip firmly. Place it on the salad. Place the other parts of the strip around the rolled peel. The tomato strip should now look like a real rose. Looks good on a sour cream or mayonnaise dressing salad.

Fruit Bowls: Make a deep 'V' cut in the centre of watermelon. To do this, make about 2" slant cut first & then another one a little away from the first one, but which meets at the bottom forming a 'V'. Continue cutting in the same way all around the melon to get a VVVV edge when the two pieces are separated. When cutting, keep the knife tilted and go deep inside. Separate the two pieces. Make the piece hollow, keeping a little red border showing. Cover the empty bowl with a plastic wrap and refrigerate. Fill salad in it at serving time. You may add some chopped watermelon pieces to the salad. Do not add too much watermelon to the salad or you may end up serving a fruit salad.

Salad Garnishes

Carrot & Radish Tuberoses

Spring Onion Flowers

Chilli Flower   ### Capsicum Basket

Tomato Rose

Fruit Bowls

Crispy Spinach & Feta Salad

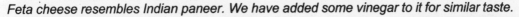

Feta cheese resembles Indian paneer. We have added some vinegar to it for similar taste.

Serves 4-6   *Picture on cover*

250 gm spinach leaves (2 cups)
1 small cucumber (kheera), 1 onion - cut into 8 pieces and separated
1 large tomato - cut into 4, remove pulp and chop into very small pieces
5-6 leaves of lettuce - tear into small pieces or ½ cup cabbage- chopped

DRESSING
3 tbsp oil, preferably olive oil
1 tsp vinegar, ¾ tsp salt, ½ tsp pepper, ½ tsp oregano (dried), 1 tbsp milk

TOPPING (MIX TOGETHER)
½ cup roughly mashed (crumbled) paneer, ¼ tsp salt, ¼ tsp pepper, 1 tbsp vinegar

1. Wash spinach leaves. Remove stalk. Pat dry leaves on a clean kitchen towel. Keep aside for 30 minutes.

2. Heat oil in a kadhai, deep fry few leaves at a time. Fry leaves carefully (oil splutters!) in 5 batches till crisp & dark green. Do not let them turn brown while frying. Drain on paper napkins with a pair of tongs (chimta). Keep aside & not in the fridge but outside, till further use. (Fried leaves turn limp in the fridge!)

3. Remove bitterness of the cucumber. Cut lengthwise into two halves. With the help of a scooper or the back of a teaspoon, remove the seeds from the cucumber by pulling the spoon straight down the length of the cucumber half. This way you get a groove in the cucumber piece.

4. Cut the cucumber into ½" thick, half-moon slices.

5. Put all ingredients of dressing in a big bowl. Mix well with a wire whisk or fork.

6. Except for the fried spinach, add all the chopped vegetables to the bowl. Mix well. Transfer to the serving bowl. Keep salad aside in the fridge to chill.

7. Mix all ingredients of topping in a bowl. Keep aside till serving time.

8. At serving time, add fried spinach to the salad, mix gently. Sprinkle topping mixture over the salad. Serve.

◀ *Italian Sour Cream Salad : Recipe on page 53*

Red Bean & Chickpea Salad

Picture on page 22   *Serves 8-10*

½ cup rajmah (red kidney beans)
½ cup safeed/kabuli channas (chickpeas)
1 cup grapes (black or green) or 1 cup peeled pieces of orange
1 small capsicum - thinly sliced, 1 onion - thinly sliced
2 tomatoes - deseeded and thinly sliced

DRESSING
4 tbsp mango chutney (use ready-made or home made)
4 tbsp olive oil, 1 tbsp honey
¼ cup chopped coriander leaves, 1 tbsp crushed garlic, 2 green chillies - chopped

1. Soak rajmah and channa for 2 hours in hot water.
2. Put rajmah, channa, 1 cup water and ½ tsp salt in a pressure cooker. Pressure cook to give 1 whistle. Reduce heat and cook for 4-5 minutes. Do not cook longer. Remove from fire. Let the pressure drop by itself. Drain.
3. Place boiled rajmah, channa, grapes or orange, capsicum, onion and tomatoes in a bowl. Mix well.
4. Place all the ingredients of the dressing in a mixer and blend to a smooth puree.
5. Pour the dressing over the salad and mix well. Chill for 1 hour and serve chilled.

Corn in Cup

Serves 6-8

1½ cups tinned corn kernels (see note), 2 tbsp butter
½ tsp salt, ½ tsp chaat masala
½ tsp red chilli flakes or ¼ tsp red chilli powder, 1 tbsp lemon juice or to taste

1. Melt butter in a kadhai. Add corn, salt, chaat masala and red chilli flakes. Stir for 2 minutes. Add lemon juice, mix well and remove from fire.
2. Serve warm immediately. Serve hot in small plastic cups or bowls.

Note: You can use fresh corn also, but with tinned corn the taste will be much better. When boiling fresh corn, do not add salt while boiling as this will harden corn kernels. Add sugar and haldi to the water and boil corn in it for 5 minutes. Add salt after removing from fire. Let corn be in hot salted water for 10 more minutes and then strain.

Lotus Stem & Guava Salad

Lotus stem can be very troublesome at times because of the dirt stuck inside the holes. To avoid the cleaning hassle, buy lotus stem which is closed at both ends. The closed ends prevent the dirt going inside the stem and you get clean white slices when you cut it.

Serves 4   Picture on page 4

200-250 gm bhein or kamal kakri (lotus stem) - peel, cut into thin diagonal slices (about 2 cups)
3- 4 tbsp cornflour
oil for frying
1 white amrood (guava)
1 pink amrood (guava)

DRESSING
2 tbsp olive oil, 1 tbsp lemon juice
1 tsp chaat masala
½ tsp salt, ¼ tsp sugar, ¼ tsp red chilli powder

GARNISH
1 green chilli - deseeded and sliced into thin long pieces
½ tbsp raw ginger juliennes or thin match stick like pieces

1. Heat oil for deep frying in a kadhai.
2. Cut lotus stem into ¼" thin diagonal slices and pat dry with a cloth.
3. Sprinkle cornflour, a pinch of salt and a pinch of pepper over the lotus stem (kamal kakri). Mix well to coat the slices.
4. Deep fry till crisp. Remove on paper.
5. Cut apple and amrood with the peel into cubes.
6. Put all ingredients of the dressing in a big bowl. Mix well with a fork.
7. Add lotus stem and amrood. Mix gently. Serve.

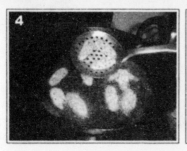

Russian Salad

Chicken and pineapple tidbits go well together. For vegetarians, omit chicken and add 1 potato, cut into small pieces and boiled in salted water.

Picture on page 93   *Serves 4-6*

300 gms chicken with bones or 1 potato
1 tbsp vinegar, 1 tbsp oil
½ cup peas (matar)
2 carrots - diced neatly into small cubes (1½ cups)
8-10 french beans - chopped (½ cup)
½ capsicum - cut into thin long pieces (juliennes)
4-5 slices of pineapple (tinned), salt and pepper to taste
5-6 crisp lettuce leaves - chill leaves in a bowl of water for 2 hours to turn crisp

DRESSING
¾ cup ready made or home made mayonnaise, recipe on page 88
¼ cup fresh cream, 1 cube cheese - grated (4 tbsp) or 1 tbsp cheese spread
½ tsp salt, ½ tsp pepper

1. To boil chicken breast, put it with ½ cup water and ½ tsp salt in a pressure cooker. Pressure cook to give 1 whistle and simmer on low heat for 3-4 minutes. Remove from fire. Remove meat from bones and cut into small pieces. Put in a bowl and sprinkle 1 tbsp vinegar and oil on it. Keep aside for 15 minutes. If using potatoes, peel and cut potato into ½" pieces and boil in salted water. Drain, pat dry potatoes with a kitchen towel. Marinate them with oil and vinegar too.

2. Boil 2 cups water with ½ tsp salt. Add peas. As soon as the boil returns, keep boiling for 2 minutes or till peas are tender. Add the beans and carrots and boil further for 1 minute only. Remove from fire and strain. Add fresh water and strain again. Keep vegetables aside.

3. Mix mayonnaise, cream, cheese spread, salt and pepper. Mix well.

4. Squeeze pineapple slices well to remove excess syrup. Chop finely.

5. Add shredded chicken or potato, chopped pineapple, boiled vegetables and capsicum to the mayonnaise. Mix well.

6. Taste and adjust seasonings if needed. Add more pepper if required. Keep aside till serving time.

7. To serve, add a little milk to the salad if it appears extra thick. Arrange lettuce on a flat or a shallow serving platter. Pile the salad in the platter, forming a pyramid (heap). Serve chilled.

Note: The left over tinned pineapple can be stored in a plastic or steel box in the freezer of the refrigerator for 2-3 months.

Broccoli Salad

Serves 4

1 small flower (125 gms) broccoli (hari gobhi) - cut into small sized florets
1 medium apple
1 tomato - cut into 4 pieces, remove seeds and chop into small pieces
1 capsicum - chop into small pieces
1 onion- chopped

DRESSING
¼ cup cream
¼ cup tomato sauce
1 tbsp lemon juice, 1 tbsp soya sauce
½-1 tsp sugar (depending on taste)
½ tsp salt, 1 tsp pepper powder
6-8 flakes of garlic
2 tbsp chopped coriander leaves
2 tbsp chopped mint leaves (poodina)

1. Cut broccoli into very small florets with long stalks.
2. Boil 2 cups water in a large pan. Add ¾ tsp salt and ½ tsp sugar to the water. Add broccoli pieces to the boiling water. Bring to a boil again. Drain immediately and rinse in cold water to prevent further cooking.
3. In a small mixer put all ingredients of dressing. Churn well for 2 minutes. Keep dressing aside in the mixer itself.
4. Chop the apple alongwith the peel into very small pieces. In a bowl mix broccoli, apple, tomato, capsicum and onion.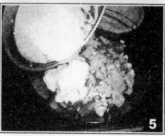
5. Pour the prepared dressing on the vegetables and mix well. Check salt and pepper.
6. Transfer to a serving bowl. Chill in the fridge till serving time.
7. To serve, mix the salad well with two forks. Garnish with a tomato rose and fresh coriander or mint sprigs. Serve chilled.

Note: Instead of broccoli, cauliflower can be used. You can top the salad with some roasted almonds or walnuts also.

Potato, Apple & Celery Salad

Picture on page 75   *Serves 5-6*

12 baby potatoes, choose really tiny ones or 1 big potato
3 large, red apples (delicious) - cut into ½" cubes without peeling
3-4 stalks celery - cut into ¼-½" slices (½ cup)
3-4 tbsp chopped walnuts (akhrot)
1 tbsp lemon juice
1 tbsp oil
salt & pepper to taste
¾ cup mayonnaise, eggless mayonnaise is available in bottles

GARNISH
2-3 lettuce leaves

1. Wash and peel baby potatoes. In the absence of baby potatoes, make balls of a big potato with the help of a melon scooper.

2. Place potatoes in a sauce pan with 4-5 cups water and 2 tsp salt. Bring to a boil. Cover and cook on low heat for 10 minutes, till potatoes turn soft. Remove from fire and strain.

3. Transfer to a mixing bowl. Cut the unpeeled apples into ½" cubes and mix with the potatoes in the bowl.

4. Chop the celery stem as shown (only stem is used). Add celery stalks.

5. Add ½ tbsp oil and lemon juice immediately, so that the apples do not discolour.

6. Add salt and pepper and toss gently to mix well. Cover with a cling film and chill covered for 1-2 hours or till serving time.

7. Before serving, add the walnuts and pour the mayonnaise. Add ½ tbsp oil. Mix gently. Check seasoning.

8. To serve, fill half bowl with salad. Arrange 2-3 lettuce leaves on a side. Fill the bowl with the left over salad.

Crisp Okra & Grape Salad

A very refreshing salad with a Mediterranean dressing of chick-peas flavoured with fresh herbs like mint and fenugreek. When fresh fenugreek leaves are unavailable, use half the quantity of dried fenugreek (kasoori methi).

Serves 4-6

500 gm bhindi (okra) - cut into diagonal slices
2 tbsp cornflour, oil for frying
1 potato - boiled, peeled and cut into small cubes
1 cup green and 1 cup black grapes - halved

DRESSING
2 tbsp oil
3 tbsp kabuli/safeed channas (chickpeas) - soaked in warm water for 3 hrs or more
2 tbsp poodina (mint leaves)
¼ cup fresh methi leaves (fenugreek leaves)
2 tbsp lemon juice, 2 tsp sugar, ½ tsp salt to taste, 1 tsp red chilli flakes
¼ cup curd

1. Soak channas overnight in tap water or for 2-3 hours in warm water. Measure ¼ cup of soaked channas.
2. Grind ¼ cup soaked channas alongwith all the other ingredients of the dressing to a smooth sauce. Keep aside.
3. Wash and pat dry bhindi.
4. Cut bhindi into diagonal slices.
5. Sprinkle dry cornflour over it. Mix well.
6. Heat oil in a kadhai. Fry the bhindi on medium flame till crisp. Do not make it brown by frying in very hot oil. Remove from oil on paper napkins. Let it cool down to room temperature.
7. At serving time, place bhindi, potatoes and grapes in a serving bowl. Sprinkle salt and pepper over it. Pour the dressing over the salad & mix well. Check salt and serve immediately at room temperature.

Kimchi Salad

The popular Chinese salad. It is always served at the start of a Chinese meal in most Chinese restaurants. The cabbage is almost raw (just blanched) with a spicy, sweet and sour dressing.

Serves 4

½ of a medium cabbage
2 tsp salt, 2 tsp sugar
2 tsp soya sauce, 1 tsp vinegar
2 tbsp tomato ketchup
½ tsp salt and ¼ tsp pepper, or to taste
¼ tsp ajinomoto

GRIND TOGETHER TO A PASTE
2 dry red chillies - deseeded and soaked in water for 10 minutes
1 tsp chopped ginger, 1 tsp chopped garlic

1. Cut cabbage into 1½" square pieces.
2. Boil 4-5 cups of water with 2 tsp salt and 2 tsp sugar. Add cabbage to boiling water. Remove from fire immediately. Strain and refresh the cabbage in cold water. Leave it in the strainer for 15 minutes for the water to drain out completely.
3. Drain the red chillies. Grind red chillies with ginger and garlic to a rough paste using a little water.
4. To the red chilli paste, add soya sauce, vinegar, tomato ketchup, salt, pepper and ajinomoto.
5. Add the paste to the cabbage and toss lightly so that the paste coats the cabbage. Serve at room temperature.

Red Hot Mushrooms

A warm and spicy winter salad.

Serves 4

200 gm button mushroom (fresh) - cut each into 2 pieces
1 large onion - cut into 12 pieces, 1 large capsicum - cut into 1" pieces
1 tbsp oil

DRESSING
2 tbsp oil, 1½ tbsp garlic chopped
1 tsp jeera (cumin seeds), 1 tsp saboot dhania (coriander seeds)
3 dry red chillies (whole dried) - deseed a little
3 tbsp tomato ketchup, ½ tsp salt, 2 tbsp milk

1. Wash and pat dry mushrooms. Trim the stem and cut each mushroom into two.
2. For dressing, place all ingredients of dressing in a mixer and blend to a paste. Cut onion and capsicum. Keep all vegetables aside till serving time.
3. To serve, heat 1 tbsp oil in a non stick pan. Add the onion, mushrooms and capsicum. Saute on low heat for 2 minutes. Remove from fire to serving bowl.
4. Pour dressing over the sauteed vegetables. Mix gently. Serve warm or at room temperature.

Greek Salad

Serves 4-6

1½ cups shredded red cabbage, 1 cup ice berg lettuce - torn into small pieces
200 gm paneer - cut into 1" cubes
8-10 green olives - cut each into 2, 1 tomato - deseeded and thinly sliced

DRESSING
4 tbsp cream, 4 tbsp curd, 1 tbsp lemon juice
1 tbsp mustard paste, ½ tsp salt ¼ tsp pepper

TO GARNISH
1 slice bread cubes - fried to make croutons (page 11), 2 tbsp roasted peanuts

1. In a bowl place cabbage, paneer, lettuce, olives and tomatoes. Mix.
2. Gently mix all the ingredients of the dressing and pour over the salad. Mix well. Chill in the fridge till serving time.
3. Take out 15 minutes before serving from fridge, mix gently. Serve topped with fried bread croutons and peanuts.

Cole Slaw

The preferred accompaniment to most Continental food.

Serves 4-6

2 cups shredded green cabbage
½ cup shredded red cabbage, if unavailable, take ½ cup more of green cabbage
1 small onion - chopped finely
1 large carrot - grated thickly
2-3 slices pineapple or 1 orange - skinned, peeled and cut into ½" pieces
a few black grapes, optional
¾ cup mayonnaise, eggless mayonnaise is available in bottles
4 tbsp cream

VINAIGRETTE DRESSING
2 tbsp vinegar
4 tbsp olive oil or any cooking oil
1 tsp mustard powder
¼ tsp salt, ¼ tsp sugar, ¼ tsp pepper powder

1. Mix all the ingredients of the vinaigrette dressing together in a small bowl. Mix well with a ballon-whisk or fork.
2. Remove the hard core of the cabbage and shred very finely with a sharp knife or in a food processor. Use the outer green leaves also as they are very firm and dark in colour.
3. Mix cabbage and onion in a salad bowl. Pour the vinaigrette dressing over and chill covered in the refrigerator for 4-5 hours.
4. After 4-5 hours, drain any vinaigrette dressing at the bottom of the bowl.
5. Add carrot, pineapple or orange and grapes to the salad bowl.
6. Pour mayonnaise and cream over and mix gently.
7. Taste the coleslaw for seasoning and add salt, pepper and mustard according to taste. Serve chilled.

Shredding of Cabbage

To shred cabbage, cut cabbage into 4 pieces. Remove the hard core. Place a flat side of the ¼ head of cabbage on a cutting board. Cut into thin slices with a large sharp knife. Cut slices several times to make smaller pieces.

Green Papaya Salad

The popular Thai salad with a chilli-tamarind dressing. Choose a hard, raw papaya with a white flesh. Even a slightly ripe papaya with an orangish flesh is not suitable for this salad.

Serves 4-6

3 cups grated hard, raw papaya (kachha papita)
1 tomato - cut into 8 pieces and deseeded
½ cup tender green beans (French beans or lobia or chawli) - sliced very finely
¼ cup roasted peanuts (moongphali)- crushed coarsely

TAMARIND-CHILLI DRESSING
1 tbsp tamarind pulp (imli pulp), soak a tiny marble size ball of tamarind in ¼ cup warm water and extract pulp
1 tbsp Soya sauce
2 tbsp lemon juice
2 tbsp sugar
½ tsp chilli powder, ½ tsp salt, or to taste
2 tbsp finely chopped coriander

CRUSH TOGETHER
3-4 red or green chillies and 1 flake garlic

1. Crush together red or green chillies with garlic to a rough paste. Mix this paste with all the other ingredients of the tamarind-chilli dressing in a flat bowl.
2. Peel and grate papaya from the biggest holes. Add chopped vegetables and papaya to the dressing in the flat dish. Mix well. Cover with a cling film and chill for at least one hour, so that the flavours penetrate.
3. To serve, mix in half the peanuts. Serve topped with rest of the roasted peanuts.

Cheesy Tomato Boats

Fresh cottage cheese stuffed in tomato shells.

Servings 4

2 firm big, longish tomatoes, 50 gms paneer - grated (4 tbsp)
1 tbsp chopped parsley or coriander, 1 tsp finely chopped onion, optional
½ tsp grated ginger (a small piece - grated)
3-4 black saboot kali mirch (peppercorns) - crushed
1 tsp roughly crushed roasted peanuts, ¼ tsp salt, or to taste
a few olives, optional - to garnish
some parsley or coriander - to garnish

1. Cut the tomatoes into two halves. Remove pulp with a knife neatly, leaving the walls intact. Rub some salt inside and keep them inverted for a few minutes.
2. Gently mix grated paneer with all the other ingredients.
3. Stuff into the tomato shells and press well. Cut into 2 pieces with a sharp knife.
4. Garnish each boat with a slice of olive and a coriander or parsley leaf, sprinkled with crushed black pepper corns.
5. At the time of serving warm in an oven or microwave.

Honey Chilli Sprouts

A Chinese salad.

Servings 6

4 cups moong sprouts, preferably long Chinese sprouts
2 tsp honey, 1 tbsp lemon juice or vinegar, 2 tbsp oil
2 tsp soya sauce
½ tsp red chilli paste (soak 2-3 dry red chillies in water and grind to a rough paste)
4-5 saboot kali mirch (peppercorns) - crushed
1 tomato - chopped finely
1½" piece ginger - finely grated
½ tsp salt, or to taste
greens of 1 spring onion - sliced diagonally

1. Steam the sprouts by placing them in a large stainless steel strainer (colander) on a pan of boiling water for 1 minute till crisp tender. Remove from heat.
2. Transfer sprouts to a kitchen towel. Put them in a mixing bowl.
3. Add all the other ingredients and toss well. Add more lemon juice and honey if required.

Non-Vegetarian SALADS

How to boil & shred chicken for salads?

To do so, put a chicken breast in a pressure cooker with ½ cup water. Pressure cook to give 2 whistles and then keep on low heat for 2 minutes. Remove from fire. After the pressure drops, break the meat into small pieces. 1 chicken breast will give about ½ cup cooked chicken.

Hawaiian Chicken Salad

Serves 4

250 gm boneless chicken or 300 gms chicken with bones
4 slices of pineapple - cut into 1" pieces
1 onion - sliced
5-6 leaves of iceberg
lettuce - torn into pieces

DRESSING
5 tbsp mayonnaise
¼ tsp pepper, 1 tbsp milk
1½ tbsp hot & sweet tomato chilli sauce (maggi)

1. Place the chicken pieces in a pressure cooker with ½ cup water and ¼ tsp salt, pressure cook to 2 whistles. Keep on low heat for 1-2 minutes. Remove from heat. When the pressure drops, drain chicken and cut into ½" long pieces. If using chicken with bones then remove bones from meat.
2. Mix all ingredients of the dressing in a bowl. Add chicken and mix well. Chill in the fridge till serving time.
3. At the time of serving, pat dry lettuce on a clean napkin. Mix lettuce, pineapple, onion to the chicken in dressing. Mix well and chill for 10 minutes. Serve chilled.

Thai Mince Salad

Serves 3-4

200 gms chicken mince (keema)
5 tbsp oil, preferably olive oil
1 onion- cut into round slices and separated into rings
1 tbsp crushed and chopped garlic
2 spring onions
1 large yellow or green capsicum - cut into 1" square pieces

DRESSING
5- 6 basil leaves or ½ tsp dried basil
1 tbsp soya sauce
½ tsp honey
1 tbsp vinegar (brown)
1 tsp red chilli flakes, ½ tsp salt, ½ tsp pepper

1. Cut bulb of spring onions into circles and the greens into 1" long, diagonal pieces.
2. Heat oil in a pan, add onion rings and garlic. Cook for 1 minute.
3. Add mince. Bhuno for 4-5 minutes on low medium heat till mince gets cooked. Remove from fire.
4. To the onions and mince in the pan, immediately add spring onions along with greens and capsicum. Remove from fire. Mix very well. Arrange in a salad bowl.
5. Mix all the ingredients of the dressing in a small bowl and keep aside.
6. At serving time, pour the dressing over the salad mixture. Mix well and serve cold, at room temperature or warm, according to your liking.

Chatpata Salad

Serves 5

250 gms boneless chicken
1 small cucumber - chopped
1 small tomato - remove pulp and chop
1 medium sized apple - chopped
1 large potato - boiled & chopped

DRESSING
4 tbsp mayonnaise (readymade)
4 tbsp milk
½ tsp black salt (kala namak)
½ tsp roasted jeera (cumin) - powdered
2 tbsp sweet mango chutney (you can use readymade or home-made)
2 tbsp lemon juice, 1½ tsp chat masala

1. Cut chicken into ¼" small square pieces.
2. Place the chicken pieces in a pressure cooker, add 1 cup water and ¼ tsp salt. Cover and pressure cook to give 1-2 whistles and simmer for 2-3 minutes. Remove from fire. Let the pressure drop by itself. Strain through a sieve.
3. In a bowl mix chopped chicken, cucumber, tomato, apple and potato nicely.
4. Mix all the ingredients of the dressing well in a mixer. Churn for 1 minute.
5. Pour the dressing over the salad mix in the bowl. Mix well and keep aside to chill in the fridge till serving time. Mix well before serving.

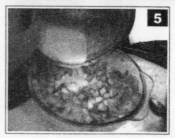

Caesar Salad with Chicken

For a vegetarian version, use a small cucumber cut into slices instead of boiled chicken.

Picture on facing page   *Serves 4*

½ bunch lettuce leaves (50 gm)
1 large chicken breast
2 hard boiled eggs
1 large tomato - deseeded & cut into thin long pieces

STIR FRIED GARLIC CROUTONS
2 slices of 1 day old white bread, 2 tsp butter
2-3 flakes garlic - crushed, 4-6 peppercorns - crushed

GARNISH
2 tbsp parmesan cheese (optional)

DRESSING
2 tbsp vinegar or wine vinegar, 1 tbsp lemon juice, 2 flakes garlic - crushed finely
6 tbsp olive oil, ¾ tsp salt, ¼ tsp black pepper powder
1 tsp sugar, 1 tsp mustard paste or powder

1. Place the chicken breast in a pressure cooker with ½ cup water and ¼ tsp salt. Pressure cook to give 1-2 whistles and then remove from heat. Cool. Chop the breast into small pieces. Put the chicken pieces in a small bowl.
2. Wash the lettuce and discard the outer hard leaves. Tear the tender leaves into small pieces. Soak in chilled water.
3. Mix all the ingredients of the dressing in a small bottle or mixer and shake well.
4. Pour dressing over the chicken pieces in the bowl. Mix well. Cover and refrigerate.
5. To make croutons, mix butter with garlic and peppercorns and spread on one side of the slice. Remove the sides of the bread and cut into small cubes. Cook them in an ungreased non stick pan over medium heat for 5-7 minutes, stirring frequently, till golden brown. Remove from pan and keep aside.
6. Hard boil eggs by boiling them for 8-10 minutes in water. Remove from hot water & immediately put in cold water to prevent the formation of a black ring around the yolk. Cool, shell & cut each egg into 4 slices lengthwise. Keep aside.
7. At serving time, roll the lettuce leaves in a clean kitchen towel to dry. Mix lettuce leaves, tomatoes, eggs and croutons in a large salad bowl. Pour the dressing along with the chicken pieces on the vegetables etc. Toss gently with a fork. Garnish with cheese. Serve at once.

Potato, Apple and Celery Salad : Recipe on page 64, Caesar Salad with Chicken ➢

Chicken Chaat

Serves 3-4　　　　*Picture on opposite page*

1 onion- cut into half and then into rings to get half rings
1 tomato - cut into 4 pieces, remove pulp and chop finely
1-2 green chillies - deseeded and chopped finely
1 tbsp chopped coriander
1 tsp butter
1 tsp maida
1 tsp lemon juice
¼ tsp pepper, ½ tsp chat masala
½ tsp bhuna jeera powder (roasted cumin powder)
few cabbage leaves - dipped in chilled water for 15 minutes

BOIL TOGETHER
175 gms boneless chicken breast
1 tej patta (bay leaf), 2 saboot kali mirch (peppercorns), 2 laung (cloves)
1 maggi chicken stock cube - crumble with your hands

1. Place the chicken in a pressure cooker, add tej patta, saboot kali mirch, laung and 1 cup water. Crumble 1 stock cube and add to the chicken. Cover and pressure cook to give 2 whistles and simmer for 2-3 minutes. Remove from fire. Let the pressure drop by itself. Strain through a sieve, reserving the stock.

2. Cut chicken into thin long slices. Keep aside.
3. Heat butter in a non stick pan. Add sliced chicken, stir fry till chicken gets golden brown from various sides.
4. Add maida and stir fry for a minute.

5. Add the reserved 1 cup stock, mix. Cook covered for about 7- 8 minutes till the stock turns almost dry, but still saucy so that it can coat the vegetables.
6. Add lemon juice, pepper, chat masala and bhuna jeera. Remove from fire. Let it come to room temperature.
7. Add onion, tomato, green chilli and chopped coriander. Mix well. Check salt.

8. Arrange cabbage leaves in a shallow bowl. Pour the salad in the centre of the bowl. Chill till serving time.
9. At serving time, mix chaat gently with the help of 2 forks. Decorate with fresh coriander leaves. Serve chilled.

Salad Nicoise

A French salad with tuna. The word "Nicoise" is pronounced as ni-SWAH.

Serves 3-4

200 gm canned tuna - drained and flaked into 1½" pieces
4-5 lettuce leaves - roughly torn and dipped in chilled water
1 tomato - cut into 8 pieces
1 potato - boiled and cut into 8 slices lengthwise
4-6 french beans - threaded and boiled till crisp-tender, keep whole
6-8 round slices of cucumber
1 tbsp pickled capers, optional, (you get them pickled in bottles like olives)
1 tbsp chopped parsley
6 black olives
1 egg - hard boiled and cut into 4 pieces lengthwise - to garnish

CREAMY HONEY MUSTARD VINAIGRETTE
1½ tbsp vinegar, 6-7 tbsp olive oil
1 tsp powdered sugar, 2 tsp mustard paste, 1 tsp honey
½ tsp salt & ¼ tsp pepper, or to taste
2 tbsp chopped fresh herbs - fennel or dill or mint or parsley
2 tbsp fresh cream

1. For the honey mustard vinaigrette dressing, put all ingredients except fresh herbs and cream, into a deep bowl. Mix well with a whisk or you can put all ingredients together in a bottle, replace the lid securely and give the bottle a really good shake. Mix until the dressing has lightly emulsified. Store, covered, in the refrigerator. Before using, bring the jar to room temperature for atleast 30 minutes before the dressing is needed and shake again.

2. When needed, add cream and 2 tbsp chopped fresh herbs such as dill, fennel or mint for a stronger flavour and shake up in the dressing.

3. At the time of serving, wrap the lettuce leaves in a clean kitchen towel to pat dry the leaves well.

4. Put leaves at the bottom of the serving bowl. Pour 1 tbsp dressing on them.

5. Put green beans, cucumber, potatoes and tomatoes also. Pour all the dressing.

6. Top with capers, tuna (drained and flaked), black olives, parsley. Lightly toss.

7. Garnish with eggs.

Thousand Island Tomatoes

A delicious salad, looks beautiful when placed in the centre of the table.

Serves 8   *Picture on backcover*

8 small tomatoes
1 chicken breast - boiled & shredded into tiny pieces
2 tinned pineapple slices - squeezed & cut into tiny pieces
2 tbsp shredded green or red cabbage

THOUSAND ISLAND DRESSING
3 tbsp mayonnaise
1 tbsp thick cream
1 tbsp ready made tomato puree
a few drops of tabasco sauce
¼ tsp pepper, salt to taste
1 tsp very finely chopped onion, 1 tsp very finely chopped capsicum

1. Wash chicken. Pressure cook with ½ tsp salt and ½ cup water to give one whistle.
2. Debone the meat and shred it into small pieces.
3. Wash and dry tomatoes. Cut a slice from the top and scoop out the pulp carefully.
4. Sprinkle salt and pepper inside the tomato. Rub the salt inside. Keep them upside down.
5. Mix together - mayonnaise, cream, tomato puree, tabasco, salt and pepper to taste in a bowl.
6. Cut pineapple slices in small pieces. Squeeze gently to remove excess syrup.
7. Mix pineapple pieces, shredded chicken, cabbage, chopped onion and capsicum in a big bowl.
8. Pour the prepared dressing over the chopped vegetables and chicken in the bowl. Mix well.
9. Fill the tomatoes with the mixture.
10. Decorate on a bed of salad leaves. Serve chilled.

Note: Boiled prawns can be used instead of chicken.

Chatpata Egg Salad

Serves 6

4 hard boiled eggs
2 potatoes - boiled and each cut into 8 pieces
4-5 cabbage leaves (fresh and green) - cut into 1" square pieces
1 green chilli - deseeded and finely chopped
1 onion - finely chopped, 2-3 tbsp finely chopped coriander

DRESSING
1 tbsp tamarind (imli) pulp - soak a marble sized ball of tamarind in ¼ cup hot
water and squeeze to get 1 tbsp pulp
4 tbsp tomato ketchup
1 tsp chat masala, ½ tsp black salt, ½ tsp chilli powder, ½ tsp salt
½ tsp roasted cumin powder (bhuna jeera powder)

1. Boil water in a pan with 3-4" water in it. Put eggs in boiling water. Boil for 10-12 minutes. Remove from fire. Put the eggs in tap water immediately.

2. Peel and cut each boiled egg into 4 long pieces.

3. Heat 2 tbsp oil in a pan. Rotate the pan to cover the base of the pan with oil. Return to fire. Place potatoes in a single layer in the pan and pan fry the potatoes till crisp and golden brown on all sides. Do not stir the potatoes too much while making them crisp. Remove pan from fire.

4. To the potatoes in the pan, add cabbage leaves, chopped onion, green chilli and coriander. Mix well to coat vegetables with oil. Keep boiled eggs separate.

5. Put all the ingredients of the dressing in a cup. Keeping aside 1 tbsp dressing for the eggs, pour the rest of the dressing over the vegetables in the pan. Mix well and transfer to a serving bowl. Keep aside.

6. To serve, arrange the eggs on the salad. Dot each piece of egg with some dressing.

Julienne Chicken Sausage Salad

Everything is cut into thin long juliennes (match sticks) and mixed with a mustard dressing.

Serves 4-6   *Picture on page 93*

6 chicken sausages
6 baby corns, 100 gm mushrooms
1 firm tomato
½ green capsicum & ½ yellow capsicum or 1 green capsicum

DRESSING
6 tbsp oil, 2 tbsp vinegar, ½ tsp salt, ½ tsp pepper
½ tsp powdered sugar , 1 tsp mustard paste
1 tbsp chopped parsley (optional), 2-3 flakes garlic - crushed & chopped

TOPPING (OPTIONAL)
4 tbsp readymade salsa, 2 tbsp curd - beat well till smooth

1. Heat 1 tsp oil in a nonstick pan. Saute sausages for 1-2 minutes till light golden. Remove from fire. Cut into ¼" thick slices. Keep aside.
2. Deseed capsicum and cut into strips. Remove the pulp of the tomato and cut into thin strips.
3. Boil 4 cups water with 2 tsp salt and few drops of lemon juice. Add baby corns and mushrooms to the boiling water. When the boil returns, remove from fire. Strain the vegetables on a clean kitchen towel.
4. Pat dry vegetables on a clean kitchen towel. Cut baby corns diagonally from the centre and cut each mushroom into four pieces.
5. Mix sausages, mushrooms, baby corns, capsicum and tomato in a salad bowl.
6. Mix all the ingredients of the dressing well in a small mixer. Churn for 1 minute.
7. Pour the dressing over the salad mixture in the bowl. Mix well and keep aside to chill in the fridge till serving time. Mix well before serving. If you like, sprinkle the whipped curd and then top with salsa. Serve chilled.

All in One

Serves 4

200 gm chicken (boneless)
100 gms mushroom, preferably small size - each cut into four pieces
½ cup tinned corn
½ of a small cucumber (kheera) - peeled and cut into paper thin round slices
1 small tomato- cut into round slices
2 small eggs - full boiled and each cut into 4 long pieces
5-6 leaves of lettuce - torn into pieces

MARINADE

1" stick of cinnamon (dalchini) - crushed to a powder, ½ tsp salt
¼ tsp ground nutmeg (jaiphal), optional
1 tbsp balsamic or brown vinegar, 1 tbsp olive oil or salad oil

DRESSING

½ tsp white or black pepper, ½ tsp salt, ¼ tsp oregano
3 tbsp readymade mayonnaise, 1 tsp vinegar, 4 tbsp milk, 1-2 tbsp water

TOPPING

a 2" piece or a cube of cheese (cheddar)

1. Place the chicken in a pressure cooker with ½ cup water ¼ tsp salt and pressure to 2 whistles. Keep on low heat for 2 minutes. Remove from fire. Cool and strain the chicken. Cut chicken into long finger like pieces.

2. Mix all ingredients of marinade in a bowl. Divide the marinade in two bowls. In one bowl add mushrooms and marinate for 15 minutes.

3. In the remaining marinade add chicken. Keep aside for 15 minutes.

4. For dressing, mix all ingredients in a small bowl with a fork. Add enough water to get a thick pouring consistency.

5. Place lettuce in a bowl of cold water and keep in the fridge. Place all the chopped vegetables, marinated mushroom, chicken and prepared dressing in the fridge till serving time.

6. To serve, take a serving salad plate, pat dry lettuce on a clean towel and place in the centre of the plate in a heap. Spoon 1-2 tbsp dressing on it. Separately arrange everything around it in heaps - mushrooms, chicken, corn, eggs, cucumber and tomato slices.

7. With a spoon pour the dressing over the well arranged salad.

8. For topping, take a block or cube of cheese and peel the cheese with the help of a peeler to get shavings (thin long flat pieces). Top salad with cheese shavings. Serve immediately.

Smoked Chicken in Ginger Dressing

A pretty salad with a fresh taste that is easy to make. You can use 200 gms paneer cut into square pieces instead of chicken.

Serves 6

2 tbsp olive oil or regular cooking oil
200 gms chicken with bones - cut into 6 pieces or 150 gms boneless chicken - cut into 6 small pieces
4 spring onions - sliced diagonally including the greens
1 small red capsicum (red pepper) - finely sliced
1 small red or green chilli - deseeded and finely sliced
1 tbsp chopped fresh coriander (dhania)

ORANGE AND GINGER DRESSING
2 tbsp orange juice, 1 tsp finely grated fresh ginger
3 tbsp olive oil, 2 tbsp white vinegar, 2 tbsp white wine
½ tsp rai (brown mustard seeds)
1 tsp brown sugar, ¼ tsp salt and ¼ tsp pepper, or to taste

1. Heat 2 tbsp oil in a kadhai or a pan. Add chicken and cook on medium heat, stirring continuously otherwise the chicken will stick to the pan. Fry till chicken is golden from various sides. Reduce heat and cook covered for 3- 4 minutes. Sprinkle some water if required. Remove chicken from fire when it is done.
2. Pick up one piece of chicken at a time with the help of tongs and smoke on the naked gas flame to get black patches on various sides. Repeat with all the pieces. Cool. If using chicken with bones then remove chicken from the bones. You get thin long pieces of chicken.
3. Place smoked chicken, spring onions, red capsicum, chilli and coriander in a serving bowl.
4. To make dressing, place all ingredients of the dressing in a mixer. Blend for few seconds.
5. Pour the prepared dressing over the chicken mixture and mix well to combine. Cover with a plastic wrap or a plate and chill till serving time.
6. To serve, mix well with two forks and serve cold.

Pasta, Rice & Noodle
SALADS

How to Boil Pasta

(2 cups uncooked pasta will give 3½ cups boiled pasta)

To boil 2 cups pasta, boil 8 cups water with 1 tsp salt and 1 tbsp oil. Add pasta to boiling water. Stir to see that pasta is not sticking to the bottom of the pan. Boil, stirring occasionally, for about 7-8 minutes till pasta turns almost soft, but yet firm. Do not overcook. Remove from fire and leave pasta in hot water for 2-3 minutes. Strain. Leave for 5-7 minutes in the strainer for all the water to drain out. Spoon 1 tbsp olive oil on the cooked pasta to prevent it from sticking.

How to Boil Rice

(1 cup uncooked rice will give 2½-3 cups boiled rice)

Wash 1 cup rice with several changes of water till the water is clean. Keep aside. Boil 6 cups water with 1 tsp salt and 1 tbsp lemon juice in a deep pan. Add the rice to the boiling water. Boil for about 4-5 minutes till almost done. Remove from water. Strain through a big strainer or colander. Fluff with a fork to let the steam escape. Pour 2-3 cups tap water on the rice to arrest the heat otherwise sometimes the rice turns mushy. Leave rice in the strainer for 10-15 minutes. Spread the rice on a tray to turn dry.

How to Boil Noodles

(100 gm noodles will give 2½ cups boiled noodles)

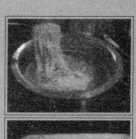

To boil 100 gms of noodles, heat 4-5 cups of water in a pan with 1 tsp salt and 1 tbsp oil. Add noodles to boiling water. Boil for 1-2 minutes till slightly undercooked. Do not cook till soft. Remove from fire. Strain and refresh in cold water immediately. Let them be in the strainer for 10 minutes for all the water to drain out. Sprinkle 1 tsp oil on them and mix well. Spread noodles on a tray covered with a cloth napkin.

Rice & Corn Salad

Serves 4

MIX TOGETHER GENTLY
¾ cup rice (long grain basmati) or 1 cup boiled rice, see page 84
1 small cucumber (kheera) - washed well and chopped with the peel (1 cup)
1 cup tinned corn kernels
1 tbsp olive oil
1 red or green capsicum - chopped
4-5 black olives or jalapenos (optional) - sliced
½ tsp salt, ½ tsp pepper, ½ tsp orgeano
2 tbsp lemon juice

TEMPERING
1 tbsp olive oil
1 onion - sliced
2-3 tbsp finely chopped parsley or basil or coriander
¼ tsp salt
1 tbsp chopped walnuts or ¼ cup thickly grated fresh coconut

OTHER INGREDIENTS
2-3 cabbage leaves - whole, dipped in a bowl of water and put in the fridge

1. To boil rice, see page *84.*
2. Chop cucumber with the peel. Keep aside.
3. To the rice, add all the ingredients written under rice. Mix well with a fork. Do not let the grains of rice break.
4. For tempering, heat oil in a non stick pan, add the onion and cook for 1 minute. Add all the other remaining ingredients. Stir for 1 minute. Remove from fire.
5. Pour this softened onion slices over the rice mixture. Mix lightly.
6. Transfer half of the salad to a serving bowl. Cut the stalk end of the cabbage leaves and pat dry on a clean kitchen towel. Arrange 2-3 cabbage leaves on the rice on any one side of the bowl such that they are about 1" above the level of the bowl. Now put the remaining salad.
7. Serve at room temperature or chill for 1 hour in the fridge. Serve garnished with chopped basil or parsley, topped with a few walnuts.

Roasted Peppers & Pasta Salad

Picture on page 40   *Serves 4*

200 gm (2 cups) pasta - bows or spirals or penne pasta
2 large green peppers (capsicums) or 1 red & 1 green pepper
1 tbsp olive oil, preferably or any other cooking oil
2-3 tbsp cream or mayonnaise
1 spring onion greens - sliced, to garnish

TOMATO DRESSING
2 tbsp olive oil, 4 flakes garlic - crushed and chopped
4 large tomatoes
1 tbsp ready made tomato puree
2 tbsp tomato sauce, 1 tbsp vinegar
1¼ tsp salt, 1 tsp oregano, a pinch of sugar, 1 tsp red chilli flakes

1. To boil pasta, see page 84.
2. Transfer boiled pasta to a bowl and pour 1 tbsp olive oil and cream or mayonnaise on it. Mix well. Keep aside.
3. Pierce a washed capsicum with a fork and hold it directly on the gas flame. Roast it on all sides for 1-2 minutes till the outer skin of capsicum gets black spots all around. Cool. Chop roasted capsicums into small pieces. Add to the pasta. Keep aside.
4. To prepare the dressing, place the tomatoes in boiling water and boil for 2-3 minutes. Remove from water and cool. Peel the tomatoes and grind in a mixer to a smooth puree. Keep fresh tomato puree aside.
5. Heat 2 tbsp oil in a pan. Reduce heat and add garlic. Stir and add the fresh tomato puree.
6. Stir for 2-3 minutes and add the ready made tomato puree, tomato sauce, vinegar, salt, oregano, sugar and chilli flakes. Stir and add ½ cup water and give one boil. Simmer for 1-2 minutes. Check the seasoning and remove from heat. Cool slightly and pour over the pasta. Toss gently. Chill in the fridge till serving time. Garnish with spring onions.

Note: The olive oil and mayonnaise or cream is added to the pasta in the beginning only to ensure that the pasta does not absorb too much dressing. However, just before serving, if the salad gets dry and the pasta sticks to each other, add a little water and toss again.

Glass Noodle Vegetable Salad

Serves 6-8

3 cups glass noodles or rice vermicelli or thin white bean threads
8-10 french beans - chopped
100 gm baby corns - sliced diagonally thinly
1 large carrot - sliced diagonally thinly
1 spring onion chopped with greens (½ cup)

DRESSING
4 tbsp oil (sesame oil, preferably)
2 tbsp light soya sauce, use less if using a dark soya sauce
1 tbsp vinegar, 2 tbsp Worcestershire sauce
2 tbsp green chilli sauce, 2 tbsp red chilli sauce
2 tbsp tomato ketchup, 1 tsp crushed garlic
¾ tsp salt, ½ tsp pepper

TO GARNISH
1 tbsp roasted peanuts (moongphali) - split into two by rolling with a rolling pin (chakla-belan)

1. To boil glass noodles, heat 4 cups of water in a pan with 1 tsp salt. Add noodles to boiling water. Remove from fire. Leave in hot water for 2 minutes or till noodles are slightly soft. Strain and refresh in cold water immediately. Let them be in the strainer for 10 minutes for all the water to drain out.
2. Again boil 2 cups water with 1 tsp salt. Add thin, diagonal slices of carrots, baby corns and french beans. When the boil returns after a minute, remove from fire. Strain immediately and refresh by adding cold water. Leave the blanched vegetables in the strainer for 15 minutes for the water to drain out completely.
2. Mix all the ingredients of the dressing. Transfer noodles to a bowl and pour ½ of the dressing over the boiled noodles. Mix well and chill in the fridge for 30 minutes.
4. Add the leftover dressing, blanched vegetables and spring onions to the noodles Mix well and chill till serving time.
5. At serving time, top with some roasted peanuts.

Chicken Noodle Salad

Boil 200 gm of cubed boneless chicken in ½ cup water and ½ tsp salt for 5 minutes or till tender. Strain. Sprinkle 1 tbsp oil and 1 tsp vinegar. Mix well and add to the salad.

Chicken Pasta Salad

Picture on page 3   *Serves 4-6*

1 cup pasta, macaroni or penne or any similar one, uncooked
150 gms chicken with bones
2 small green capsicums - cut into ½" squares

DRESSING
1 cup fresh yogurt (curd) - hang for 25- 30 minutes in a muslin cloth (mal mal kapda)
4- 5 tbsp thin cream
2¼ tbsp readymade orange squash
2 tbsp olive oil, 2 tbsp milk, ½ tsp orgeano
½ tsp pepper, 1 tsp salt
¼ tsp mustard paste, or to taste

1. To boil pasta, boil 8 cups water with 1½ tsp salt. Add pasta to boiling water. Stir to see that pasta is not sticking to the bottom of the pan. Boil, stirring occassionally, for about 10-12 minutes till pasta turns soft, but yet firm. Remove from fire and strain. Leave for 5-7 minutes in the strainer for all the water to drain out. Spoon 1 tbsp olive oil on the pasta. Keep covered in a bowl till the time of use.
2. Place the chicken pieces, bay leaf and salt in a pressure cooker with 7 cups of water. Pressure cook to give 2 whistles. Simmer for 2-3 minutes, remove and cool. Pick up the chicken pieces from the stock. (You can reserve and store the stock for any soup). Cool. Debone the meat from the bones. Discard the bones, and bay leaf. Cool. Shred finely. Let it cool. Remove bones from the chicken. Shred into very small pieces.
3. Mix the shredded chicken, capsicum, and boiled pasta in a bowl.
4. For the dressing, beat all the ingredients of the dressing in a small bowl till smooth.
5. Add the dressing to the pasta in the bowl.
6. Toss well using 2 forks. Check salt and pepper. Mix well. Serve cold.

Note: You can make this salad without chicken also. Instead of chicken use 200 gms of paneer, cut into tiny cubes. Omit step 2 and proceed further in the same way.

Salad Dressings

Dressings add colour, flavour, improve palatability and appearance and are a means of combining ingredients. There are three general types of salad dressings:

MAYONNAISE (MAKES 1½ CUPS)

2 eggs
½ tsp salt, ½ tsp pepper, 1 tsp mustard powder, 2 tsp sugar
1 tbsp vinegar, 1 tbsp lemon juice
1½ cups cooking oil (use absolutely clean oil, should be unused)

1. Break eggs into the blender of your mixer. Add salt, pepper, sugar, mustard and vinegar to the eggs. Churn for a few seconds to blend all ingredients.
2. Keeping blender on, add oil slowly spoonful by spoonful, churning continuously.
3. Keep adding oil gradually, till the sauce starts to thicken. Once the sauce thickens slightly, keeping the blender on, pour oil in a thin stream from the cup directly in larger quantities. Churn till all the oil is used and a thick mayonnaise is ready.
4. Add lemon juice. Churn once more. Remove from mixer to a bowl. Chill for 2 hours before use.

FRENCH DRESSING OR VINIAGRETTE (MAKES ½ CUP)

2 tbsp vinegar
½ cup olive oil or any cooking oil
½ tsp French mustard or mustard powder
1 tsp salt, ½ tsp powdered sugar, ½ tsp pepper powder
2 tsp lemon juice

1. Put all ingredients in a bottle with a tight fitting lid. Shake vigourously. Refrigerate until needed. Shake again before use.

Note: Excess French dressing will make green leafy vegetables flabby.

CREAM DRESSING (MAKES 1½ CUPS)

1 cup cream - lightly beaten
½ cup olive oil
2 tbsp vinegar
1 tsp mustard, ½ tsp salt, ¼ tsp sugar
¼ tsp each red chilli powder and black pepper
1 tsp sesame seeds (til) - roasted on a griddle (tawa) till golden

1. Place all the ingredients in a bottle and shake well.

Note: Tastes good with broccoli and mushroom salad.

To Prepare Stock:

FRESH VEGETABLE STOCK (MAKES 6 CUPS)

1 onion - chopped, 1 carrot - chopped, 1 potato - chopped, 5 french beans - chopped)
½ tsp salt, 7 cups water

1. Mix all ingredients & pressure cook to give 1 whistle. Reduce heat and cook for 10-15 minutes on low heat. Remove from fire.
2. Do not mash the vegetables if a clear soup is to be prepared. Strain & use as required or store in refrigerator (freezer compartment) for about a week or till further use.

FRESH CHICKEN STOCK (MAKES 5 CUPS)

bones of 1 chicken, neck and wings
1 bay leaf (tej patta), ½ onion - chopped, ½ tsp salt

1. Place all the ingredients in a pan with 8 cups of water and bring to a boil. Reduce heat and simmer for 15-20 minutes. Strain and store in a refrigerator till further use. It can also be frozen if you want to keep it for a few days.

READY-MADE STOCK (MAKES 2½ CUPS) ... QUICK STOCK

Vegetarian or chicken soup cubes or seasoning cubes may be boiled with water and used instead of fresh stock, if you are short of time. These seasoning cubes are easily available in the market and are equally good in taste.

1 seasoning cube (extra taste), chicken or vegetarian (maggi, knorr or any other brand)
2½cups of water

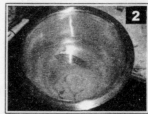

1. Crush 1 seasoning cube roughly in a pan.
2. Add 2½ cups of water. Give one boil. Use as required.

Note: The seasoning cube has a lot of salt, so reduce salt if you substitute this stock with the fresh stock. Check taste before adding salt.

Glossary of Hindi Names/Terms

Hindi or English names as used in India	English names as used in USA/UK/ Other countries
Achaar	Vegetables pickled in flavoured oil
Ajwain	Carom seeds
Aloo	Potatoes
Amchoor	Dry mango powder which makes a dish sour. 1 tsp of lemon juice can be substituted for ¼ tsp amchoor
Anjeer	Dry figs
Arhar dal	Pigeon peas
Atta	Whole wheat flour
Badaam	Almonds
Baingan	Eggplant, aubergine
Basmati rice	Fragrant Indian rice
Besan	Gram flour
Bharte waala baingan	Eggplant (aubergine) of big round variety
Bharwaan	Stuffed
Bhutta	Corn
Bhindi	Okra, lady's finger
Capsicum	Bell peppers
Chaat Masala	A spice blend (salty and sour blend)
Chaawal, Chawal	Rice
Chana dal	Split gram
Channe	Chickpeas
Chhole	Chickpeas
Chhoti Illaichi	Green cardamom
Chilli powder	Red chilli powder, Cayenne pepper
Cornflour	Corn starch
Coriander, fresh	Cilantro
Cream	Heavy whipping cream
Curd	Yogurt
Dahi	Yogurt
Dal	Pulse
Dalchini	Cinnamon
Degi mirch	Red pepper powder which is not too hot, paprika can be substituted
Dhania powder	Ground coriander seeds
Dhania saboot	Coriander seeds

Essence	Extract
French beans	Green beans
Gajar	Carrots
Garam Masala	A blend of many fragrant spices. A tsp of garam masala may be substituted by crushing 1 clove, 2-3 peppercorns and seeds of ½ black cardamom
Ghee	Clarified butter
Gobhi	Cauliflower
Haldi	Turmeric powder
Hara Dhania	Cilantro
Hari Gobhi	Broccoli
Hari Mirch	Green hot peppers, green chillies, serrano peppers
Hing	Asafoetida
Icing sugar	Confectioner's sugar
Illaichi	Cardamom
Imli	Tamarind
Jaiphal	Nutmeg
Javetri	Mace
Jeera Powder	Ground cumin seeds
Jeera	Cumin seeds
Kadhai/Karahi	Wok
Kaju	Cashewnuts
Kali dal	Black lentils
Kalonji	Nigella seeds (black oval seeds), resemble onion seeds
Karela	Bitter gourd
Kasoori methi	Dry fenugreek leaves generally used as dried herb
Katori	Individual serving bowls resembling ramekins
Keema	Mince meat
Kesar	Saffron
Khoya	Full fat milk cooked till thick. In India such cakes are available. Ricotta can be used instead
Khumb	Mushrooms
Khus Khus	Poppy seeds
Kishmish	Raisins
Kofta	Balls made from minced vegetables or meat, fried and put in a curry gravy/sauce.
Lauki	Squash
Macchi	Fish
Magaz	Melon seeds
Maida	All purpose flour, Plain flour
Makai, Makki	Corn

Russian Salad : Recipe on page 62 ➤
Julienne Chicken Sausage Salad : Recipe on page 81 ➤

Nita Mehta's BEST SELLERS (Non-Vegetarian)

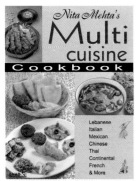

MULTICUISINE
Cookbook

THAI
cooking for the Indian kitchen

Dilli Ka Khaana

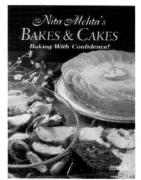

BAKES & CAKES
Baking with confidence!

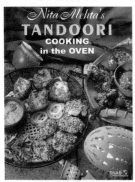

TANDOORI
COOKING

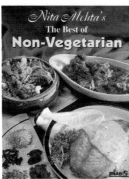

The Best of
Non-Vegetarian

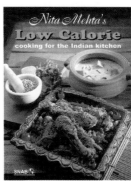

LOW CALORIE
cooking for the Indian kitchen

Tempting
SNACKS

101
MICROWAVE Recipes

MUGHLAI
Khaana

PUNJABI
Khaana

CHINESE
cooking for the Indian kitchen

MUGHLAI
Non-Vegetarian

The Best of
CHICKEN Recipes

SNACKS
Non-Vegetarian

Favourite
NON-VEGETARIAN

Nita Mehta's BEST SELLERS

SUBZIYAAN

FOOD from around the **WORLD**

QUICK Vegetarian Cooking

Different ways with **PANEER**

Great **INDIAN** Cooking

EVERYDAY Cooking

Vegetarian **SNACKS**

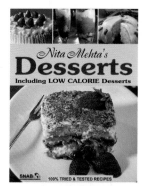

DESSERTS Including Low Calorie Desserts

Perfect Vegetarian Cookery

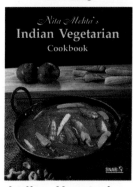

Indian Vegetarian Cookbook

Flavours of **INDIAN** Cooking

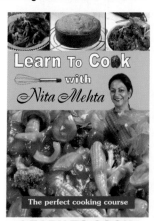

LEARN TO COOK